# The New Canadian Constitution

# The New Canadian Constitution

DAVID MILNE

James Lorimer & Company, Publishers
Toronto 1982

ISBN 0-88862-544-8 paper
     0-88862-545-6 cloth

Cover design: Brant Cowie
Cover photo: Brian Willer

---

Canadian Cataloguing in Publication Data

Milne, David A., 1941-
   The new Canadian constitution

(Canadian issues)

1. Canada.   2. Canada — Politics and government —
1980-      *  3. Canada — Constitutional history.
I. Title.   II. Series: Canadian issues (Toronto, Ont.)

JL27.M54      342.71'02      C82-094439-4

---

James Lorimer & Company, Publishers
Egerton Ryerson Memorial Building
35 Britain Street
Toronto, Ontario  M5A 1R7

Printed and bound in Canada
6  5  4  3  2  1     82  82  84  85  86  87

# Contents

To Peter H. Russell

# Preface

When I was asked to write a book on the new Canadian constitution September last, I was both interested and apprehensive. I was drawn to the project because I had been teaching in the area for many years, had participated in the summer 1980 constitutional talks and had been following later developments fairly closely. My apprehension stemmed from the fact that at that time it was by no means certain that we would have a new constitution. In the end I am grateful that events looked kindly on my labours.

The work could not have been completed without the assistance of many individuals and the support of the University of Prince Edward Island. I wish to thank in particular my colleagues in the Department of Political Science as well as the Senate Research Committee for providing assistance through the Social Sciences and Humanities Research Council of Canada general grant. In addition, I have profited enormously from the comments and encouragement of several academic readers. My thanks go out especially to Peter Russell, Alan Cairns, Richard Simeon and Arthur Ross. I am also grateful for legal opinions offered by Peter Cumming, Peter Hogg,

Brian Slattery, Marc Gold and Kent McNeil. The revised draft was also read by some of the direct participants in the constitution-making process, including J. Angus MacLean, former premier of Prince Edward Island, and Barry Toole, deputy secretary to cabinet for New Brunswick Premier Richard Hatfield. They, together with senior officials interviewed in the federal, Ontario and Quebec delegations, have provided me with valuable perspectives on many matters, but of course they bear no responsibility for the judgements I have made.

I am also grateful to Dr Catherine Wallace, chairman of the Maritime Provinces Higher Education Commission, who read the revised draft and helped improve the text at a number of points. My thanks also extend to Barb Garnham for her superb work typing the manuscript, to Patsy McQuaid for research assistance and to Jim Lorimer and his staff for their valuable and tactful advice.

Finally, I want to acknowledge Fran and Kyla without whose patience and support this book could not have been written.

Charlottetown, 1982

# Chronology: Major Events in the Constitution-Making Process, 1980-82

## 1980

| | |
|---|---|
| Feb. 18 | Return of the Liberals to power under Trudeau's leadership |
| April 15 | Official referendum campaign begins in Quebec |
| May 20 | Federalists win the Quebec referendum |
| June 9 | First ministers meet on the constitution and set up agenda of 12 topics |
| July 7-25, Aug. 25-29 | Negotiations between officials and ministers responsible for federal-provincial relations in Montreal, Toronto and Vancouver; final negotiating session in Ottawa to prepare for Conference of First Ministers |
| Sept. 7 | Quebec circulates Kirby memorandum |
| Sept. 8-12 | First Ministers' Conference in Ottawa; conference failure announced Sept. 13 |
| Oct. 6 | Federal government places unilateral resolution before Parliament |
| Oct. 14 | Premiers meet in Toronto and court challenges are announced |
| Oct. 23-24 | Closure applied and vote taken to send constitutional resolution to a Special Joint Committee |

| | |
|---|---|
| Nov. 5 | Britain's Select Committee on Foreign Affairs studies Britain's role regarding the Canadian Parliament's request |

## 1981

| | |
|---|---|
| Jan. 12 | Justice Minister Chrétien tables the government's amendments to the resolution |
| Jan. 30 | Britain's Select Committee reports that "Westminster cannot act as a mere rubberstamp on all requests coming from the Parliament of Canada" |
| Feb. 3 | Manitoba Court of Appeal supports Ottawa by a vote of 3 to 2 |
| Feb. 13 | Special Joint Committee reports to Parliament with proposed amendments; debate begins Feb. 17 |
| March 19 | Liberal House Leader Yvon Pinard gives notice of motion to limit debate |
| March 31 | Newfoundland Court unanimously declares Ottawa's unilateral resolution illegal |
| April 13 | Parti Québécois wins Quebec election |
| April 15 | Quebec Court of Appeal supports Ottawa by a vote of 4 to 1 |
| April 16 | Premiers in Gang of Eight sign Constitutional Accord in Ottawa |
| April 23 | Final amendments to the resolution adopted in the House of Commons |
| April 28– May 4 | Supreme Court of Canada hearing |
| Sept. 28 | Supreme Court brings down its judgement |
| Oct. 3 | Quebec's assembly passes a resolution denouncing federal unilateralism |
| Oct. 20 | Premiers meet in Montreal |
| Nov. 2 - 5 | First Ministers' Conference on the Constitution begins |

| Nov. 5 | Announcement of substantial federal-provincial agreement over the constitution; Premier Lévesque dissents |
| Nov. 24 | House approves amendment to the Charter of Rights strengthening the section on sexual equality |
| Nov. 26 | House approves amendment restoring "existing" aboriginal treaty rights section |
| Dec. 2 | House of Commons approves final constitutional resolution |
| Dec. 2 | Quebec refers the question of its right of veto to the Quebec Court of Appeal |
| Dec. 8 | Senate approves final constitutional resolution; Governor General Schreyer gives his assent |
| Dec. 9 | Constitutional resolution delivered to Buckingham Palace |

### 1982

| Jan. 14 | British Prime Minister Margaret Thatcher turns down Premier Lévesque's request to delay proceedings until courts have ruled on Quebec veto |
| Jan. 28 | British Court of Appeal rejects Indian claims against patriation package |
| March 8 | British House of Commons passes Canada Act |
| March 25 | House of Lords passes the Canada Act |
| March 29 | Queen Elizabeth II gives royal assent to Canada Act |
| April 7 | Quebec Court of Appeal unanimously declares that Quebec has no veto |
| April 17 | Queen Elizabeth II proclaims Canada Act |

# Introduction

Even the weather appeared to reflect the ambivalence of the nation on April 17, 1982, the date of the proclamation of Canada's new constitution. The outdoor procession of leaders and dignitaries preceding the arrival of Queen Elizabeth in an open landau enjoyed brilliant sunshine and the balmiest April temperatures in Ottawa's memory. Such a propitious setting symbolized for many Canadians satisfaction at finally bringing home the constitution and hope for the country's future. Yet as the queen began to deliver the proclamation address on an outdoor dais before the Parliament buildings, a sudden rainstorm intervened, reminding Canadians of the thousands of Quebecers and native peoples who were then receiving the constitution in protest and mourning. After the signing ceremony, the weather abruptly changed; the rain stopped — but still, as if to temper expectations, the sun did not come out.

But whatever the weather's verdict, there was no mistaking the significance of the patriation ceremony. The country's full political independence was now recognized in law, and Canadians assumed final responsibility for all their own affairs, including any changes in the basic constitutional framework of the country. But all the pomp and circumstance of this state occasion symbolized much more than the principle of full legal independence. It was the culmination of a protracted struggle to redefine the country by incorporating in Canada's fundamental law new standards of justice between the two founding peoples, of citizens' rights, and of Canadian federalism. It was only because of the stakes which governments and peoples had in the constitution, and in the process which created it, that the patriation ceremony simultaneously generated patriotic flag-waving, protest marches organized by Parti Québécois opponents in Montreal, and the mute resistance of native peoples wearing black arm bands. But in the world of Canada's constitutional politics, such an outcome should not be thought unusual. Strife and division called into being the idea of constitutional change and they have accompanied the process of constitutional renewal at every point in its history.

Canadians have long been encouraged to look to legal foundations for explanations of, and solutions to, the country's disorders. Never has this tendency been stronger than during the prime ministership of Pierre Elliott Trudeau, the one-time constitutional scholar who attributed the nation's most serious internal divisions, namely, separatism in Quebec and regional alienation in the West and Atlantic Canada, to "the inadequacies of our fundamental law" and to "lack of action" in correcting those legal flaws. Remaking Canada therefore has been seen as principally a work of renovating our legal architecture, of reforming the fundamental social contract under which the different peoples and regions of Canada live.

But such a thorough undertaking can be mounted only when threats to the state are grave enough and when grievances cannot be adequately resolved under the old constitution. After more than a hundred years of growth, Canada seemed to have arrived at such a point. During the constitutional battle Canadians were so torn between competing visions of nationalism, regionalism and federalism that our collective future together was in some doubt. The gloomy outlook of books published on Canada suggested the gravity of the situation: *Canada in Question, Option: Quebec, Must Canada Fail?, The Precarious Homestead, Unfulfilled Union, The Roots of Disunity, Canada and the Burden of Unity, Divided Loyalties, Western Separatism*. Out of this backdrop of political confusion and pessimism Canada's new constitution was created—a resolution of bitter divisions between French- and English-speaking Canadians and between the different regions in the country.

The history of the two founding peoples at best tells of an accidental and indifferent marriage and at worst of a thoroughly injurious association. Past religious bigotries and misunderstandings, along with linguistic intolerance and persecution of minorities, particularly in the English-speaking provinces and more recently in Quebec, have always marred any possibility of a genuine national partnership between the French- and English-speaking peoples. Under Confederation, for example, French language rights and schools for the French-speaking minority were extinguished in Manitoba for over three quarters of a century before the courts in 1979 declared the Manitoba legislature's actions illegal. Bans were also imposed on French language public schools elsewhere in the West, in the Maritimes and in Ontario. The subsequent assimilation of French-speaking minorities has been relentless. As for the new Quebec, even before the establishment of an officially unilingual French society in Quebec in 1976, Parti Québécois leader René Lévesque calmly speculated in 1970 about the gradual future assimilation of Quebec's anglophone minority. In fact, the sad history of what Hugh MacLennan called the "two solitudes" has given rise to two fundamental choices for Quebecers: a separatist option, which sees an independent unilingual French Quebec as the only rational way out of the impasse, and a reformed federalism option, which aims to make the whole of Canada acceptable to both founding peoples and above all to make it a safe home for linguistic minorities. These two constitutional options compete for the allegiance of Quebecers in the persons of two of her most popular native sons, René Lévesque and Pierre Trudeau. That struggle was at the heart of the politics surrounding the new constitution.

The other critical case of divided loyalties arose principally in the Atlantic and Western provinces. Confederation has not been particularly kind to the peoples of these regions, nor indeed to those in the North. Public discontent at being treated so long as hinterland areas in a federation dominated by Ontario and Quebec produced a regional politics and ideology that challenged Ottawa's right to speak for the national will. The competition between regional and national elites heated up to a higher point than ever in the late 1970s. This struggle impaired the legitimacy and representativeness of the central government, as evidenced by the West's refusal to give the Liberal party even token representation from the region in the 1980 election, and the sporadic bursts of support for Western separatism such as the election of a separatist MLA in Alberta in 1982.

In the absence of effective channels for the expression of this discontent at Ottawa, most premiers emerged as spokesmen for regionalism. By drawing on their people's grievances under Confederation, they were able to make a strong case for increased provincial rights and powers. This ran directly counter to the Trudeau government's "one Canada" strategy. Similarly the bitter feud between Quebec's federalist and nationalist elites over the future status of Quebec and of the French fact in Canada was also fought out through the constitution-making process. This conflict and that between "province building" and "nation building" formed an essential part of Canada's constitutional politics during the six years preceding the passage of the Canada Act. In the chapters that follow, the same struggle can be seen at work in all the twists and turns of the constitution-making process. As the players planned their strategies and marshalled their forces in all the different forums in which this constitutional battle was fought, the overriding issues were always the same: whether separatism, regionalism or Trudeau's "one-Canada" nationalism would win the right to shape the country in its image.

This book examines the constitution in the light of its connection to Canada's chronic problems and to the complexity of federal-provincial conflict. Chapter 1 offers a brief summary of developments prior to 1980. Chapter 2 begins with the bargaining between federal and provincial governments immediately following the defeat of the sovereignty-association option in the PQ's May 1980 referendum and ends with the breakdown of talks in September after three gruelling months of planning and negotiation. Chapter 3 focuses on the federal government's plan for unilateral action, announced in October 1980 but effectively stalled by challenges to its legality in the courts. The landmark decision of the Supreme Court on September 28, 1981, and its contribution to a final negotiated settlement is discussed in Chapter 4. Chapter 5 takes the story of the constitutional struggle through to the historic federal-provincial agreement of November 5, 1981, traces the painful aftermath with Quebec out of the agreement, and ends with the Canadian Parliament's approval of the last version of the resolution in December 1981. After reviewing the final stages of approval in the British Parliament, the concluding chapter examines the nature of the new Canadian constitution, both in terms of the interests, issues and accidents that shaped it and in terms of its own strengths and weaknesses.

Throughout the turbulent process of constitution making, the narrative attempts to explore the political and strategic issues at the bargaining table, in Parliament and in the courts of law. Such an analysis has been made immensely easier by the leak of the famous "Kirby memorandum," a lengthy federal cabinet document (in fact prepared by many officials not just Michael Kirby) that outlined the entire federal government game plan for a negotiated settlement or, failing that, for unilateral action. This document gives a direct look at constitutional planning and strategy, not to mention a rare glimpse into the federal government's style of conducting federal-provincial relations. Highlights from this document have been reprinted in Appendix 2. The exact provisions of the new Canadian constitution are reproduced in Appendix 1.

In many respects, as the following pages illustrate, the making of Canada's new constitution was not a particularly high-minded process. But then, despite the veneration usually accorded to "constitution-makers," there is really no good reason to think the reforming of a state's constitution ought to be a noble exercise. On the contrary, when bargaining politicians represent sharply different views and interests, and especially when they contain within their ranks both committed separatists and federalists, the process is much more likely to be in the tradition of Machiavelli, the Italian Renaissance statesman who taught the difficult art of political realism. Whatever achievements are won must be wrested and secured by the wiliest of tactics. The battle over the Canadian constitution is in that respect a splendid study of Machiavellian statesmanship.

But the struggle between Canada's political elites over the constitution was always more than a spectators' sport. Because the battle concerned the kind of state (or states) Canada was to be, it challenged every Canadian to define his sense of country more sharply than ever before. Predictably there was no consensus among Canadians as a whole, and debate over the constitution and the process which brought it into being is bound to continue.

However whatever their differences over the constitution, Canadians will want a final answer to the one really decisive question: Will the Canada Act succeed in preserving and improving Canada or will it send the nation headlong into more serious crises? On that question, only history can judge.

# 1
# Politics and the Constitution: An Overview

Despite the best efforts of constitutional historians to make their subject look dreary and formal, Canadian constitutional politics is fascinating. It dramatizes intergovernmental conflict over questions of power and philosophy better than any passing policy dispute could possibly do. In a federal state like Canada, constitutional politics also permits us to monitor the stresses of federal-provincial and interprovincial relations and to see the directions in which the country might move.

The constitution in a federal state forms a master power grid from which all the governmental players get their authority. Not only does it distribute legal power among legislatures, it also limits the exercise of these powers, imposes obligations upon governments and declares and enforces through the courts certain principles which thereafter bind all the players. Governments therefore are acutely sensitive to their position in the power grid and wary of proposed changes in the distribution of power or in the rules governing how changes are made. This jealous regard is not simply an expression of collective self-interest; since the constitution represents a fundamental bargain over larger moral purposes, the issue is one of principle and not merely power.

In this chapter, the interrelationships between governmental politics and the constitution are briefly examined. First is an account of the effort to patriate the constitution with an amending formula acceptable to the governments of Canada. Then the origins and development of the constitutional struggle over French-English relations, a charter of rights, and the status of Quebec in Canada are discussed. Finally, the discussion turns to regionalism in Canada and its role in the constitution-making process of 1976-82.

## Rules for Constitutional Change: The Price of Legal Independence

In effecting patriation the new Canadian constitution brought to a close a difficult and protracted struggle among governments, which began in 1927 with the first attempts to get agreement on an amending formula. The problem surfaced that year in the negotiations which led to Canada's independence as a self-governing dominion within the British Commonwealth, formally recognized by the Statute of Westminster in 1931. The issue was straightforward: how could all governments in Canada be brought to agree on a procedure for altering the constitution so that further legal recourse to Britain would be unnecessary. Prior to 1927, it had seemed perfectly acceptable to have Britain make the desired changes to the British North America Act. The convention had already developed that Britain would do so only on the request of a joint address of the House of Commons and Senate, at that time usually without consultation with the provinces. But when Canada was about to end its legal subordination to Britain, a new way of changing the constitution had to be found, and this mechanism would have to respect the federal nature of the country. When no agreement was reached by 1931, Britain retained in section 7 of the statute the legal power to change the written constitution by virtue of Canada's failure to assume it. Over the next half century, the retention of this colonial link offended Canadian legal nationalists who looked to the ritual of finally bringing home the constitution with undisguised enthusiasm.

But even then the symbolic completion of Canadian independence from Britain hid another agenda: the formal structuring of power within Canada. As fondly as any federal or provincial politician might have wished for such symbolic independence, it could not be achieved without settling, through the amending formula, who had the power to determine the constitutional future of the country. Since the actors in the negotiations were all the governments of the country, it is understandable that jockeying to advance or defend sectional interests and jurisdictions was a part of any such discussions.

That made coming to an agreement tough enough. But Canada had additional difficulties. Its history, geography, and economic, cultural and political diversity made a settlement of the power question almost insuperable. First, there was a linguistic division between the French- and English-speaking peoples, principally reflected in the partition of the country into a francophone Catholic Quebec and a predominantly English society everywhere else. Much of Canada's troubled history revolved around the history of these two peoples, especially the treatment of linguistic minorities. Secondly, there were the regional grievances over the unequal benefits and burdens of the union and the wide variations of size, power and wealth among the provinces, which tended to be reflected in demands for special treatment in any amending formula. Because Ontario and Quebec included well over half the Canadian population, it was obvious that amending formulas from federal states with populations less unequally distributed would not easily apply here. Finally, there was antagonism towards the federal government itself on the part of both the "have" and the "have-not" provinces: from the have-nots, the resentment and fear of mere dependents, and from the haves, rivalry for pre-eminence in the state.

Given these divisions, it is not surprising that conference after conference floundered on a sea of distrust and ambition. So great were these forces that amendment proposals were almost invariably complicated, requiring unanimous consent on certain key "entrenched" areas of the constitution and more flexible procedures for others. Even so, the various tortuous formulae outlined in Table 1 failed over the years to win complete agreement. Most often (in 1936, 1964, 1971, 1981), Quebec was the holdout.

The formulae cited in the table reflect delicate governmental balancing of fundamental issues bearing on constitutional amendments in a federal state. All general formulae, for example, declare that basic changes to the Confederation bargain require the consent of not just Parliament but also of a majority of provinces. In proposals forwarded after 1927, the consent of a majority of provincial governments was also required to represent at least 50 per cent of the Canadian population. In all proposed formulae, it has been the consent of *governments* — federal and provincial

—not peoples that has been the historical basis for proposals on constitutional change. Only with Prime Minister Trudeau's unilateral plan of 1980 was the suggestion of change by referenda introduced; even then the new method was advanced as a deadlock-breaking alternative to the "normal" route. Table 1 also shows that until a regionally based proposal was made by Trudeau in 1971, it was always strictly numbers of provinces that would form the basis of constitutional agreements, with no regional quotes. Also, prior to 1971 all formulae gave no single province a veto. Population requirements in formulae since 1936 then entailed the consent of Quebec *or* Ontario; changing demographic conditions might favour different provinces, but it is unlikely that shifts in population would ever permit a single province a veto.

In this way, the general formulae sought to provide flexibility for constitutional change and at the same time to enshrine the principle of equality of provinces. This could be accomplished, however, only by giving every province blocking powers on certain key matters. In the column on unanimity, it is striking that every amendment formula except the Victoria proposal set out certain vital areas that could not be changed without every province's consent. Apart from the constant inclusion of language and educational rights, and the usual listing of provincial representation in the federal houses of Parliament and the role of the monarchy, the significant pattern is the consistent demand for protection of provincial legislative powers as outlined in section 92 of the British North America Act. (Federal legislative powers would presumably not need special protection since Ottawa was a required party in any constitutional amendment formula.) At no time except during the Trudeau era

## Table 1
## CONSTITUTIONAL AMENDMENT PROPOSALS, 1927-81[1]

| Year/Formula for General Agreement | Sections Changed by Unanimity Only | Special Features/Comments |
|---|---|---|
| **1927** House of Commons, Senate, a majority of the provinces (no population requirement) | s.92 h.12[2] (solemnization of marriage) h.13 (property and civil rights) h 14 (administration of justice) s.93 (minority education rights) s.133 (French and English language guarantees) | Of provincial powers listed in section 92, marriage and justice were considered important especially to Quebec, while property and civil rights, as their most general and important source of legislative authority, were vital to all provinces. Minority rights and language guarantees hereafter fall into the "entrenched" category |
| **1936** (near agreement; newly elected Quebec Premier Duplessis dissents) House of Commons, Senate, 6 provinces having 55% of population (i.e., must include Ontario or Quebec) | All sections above s.92 h.4 (establishment of provincial offices and officers) h.5 (management and sale of public lands) h.8 (municipal institutions) | New concern over provincial representation in Parliament and the monarchy reflected in the unanimity column. In section 92 the provinces agree to permit changes in the area of property and civil rights (h.13) and local |

| | Sections | Comments |
|---|---|---|
| | h. 15 (imposition of provincial fines)<br>s.9 (role of the monarchy)<br>s.21 (number of senators)<br>s.22 (provincial representation in the Senate)<br>s.51 (House of Commons representation)<br>s.51A (minimum provincial representation in House of Commons)<br>Amending procedure | matters in the province (h. 16) without unanimity, in return for a right to "opt out." A few other items in s.92 are added to the unanimity list to compensate |
| 1950<br>not settled | All sections above<br>s.92<br>s.91 (federal powers) | Entrenchment of whole division of powers pushed by Ont. and Que. but resisted by Sask. |
| 1964 (near agreement; Quebec withdraws)<br>Fulton-Favreau formula: House of Commons, Senate, 7 provinces comprising at least 50% of population | All sections above<br>s.109 (provincial property) | Delegation[3] of powers possible between Parliament and a minimum of 4 provinces except that provinces restricted to transferring only s.92,h.6 (prisons),h.10 (local works), h.13 and 16. Only |

*Table 1 continued*

| Year/Formula for General Agreement | Sections Changed by Unanimity Only | Special Features/Comments |
|---|---|---|
| | | the power to make statutory enactments in these areas could be transferred, not jurisdiction |
| 1971 (near agreement; Quebec withdraws) Victoria formula: House of Commons, Senate, majority of provinces comprising: every province which has or had 25% of Canada's population, at least 2 provinces from both Atlantic and Western Canada (making up at least 50% of population for latter) | None | No categories for unanimity. The largest provinces—Ontario and Quebec—given a veto perpetually. "Regional" formula disguises preferred status for 2 central provinces. A provision for overriding the Senate written in |
| 1979 Alberta formula: House of Commons, Senate, 7 provinces comprising at least 50% of | Amending procedure | Reactivation of "opting out" from 1936 formula, but applying to all provincial powers and rights (s.92). Any province may block an amend- |

| | | |
|---|---|---|
| population | | ment in its jurisdiction. Equality of provinces restored. Provision for overriding Senate available |
| **1981** April 16 Constitutional Accord (Gang of Eight's slight reworking of Alberta formula) | s.9 s.51A s.133 Composition of Supreme Court Amending procedure | Financial compensation to be made for opting out or delegating powers (latter applies to provinces *and* Parliament) |
| **1981** Parliament's unilateral resolution, April 23: Victoria formula with population requirement for West deleted | None | Amendment by referenda is added wherever a federal proclamation is supported by a majority of voters, both overall and in quota of provinces as set in Victoria formula |

Notes

[1] Amendments which strictly concern the constitution of a province may, with the exception of the office of lieutenant governor, be taken unilaterally (s.92[1]). Since 1949 the same right to change the constitution as it affects exclusively federal matters was, with certain exceptions, granted to the Parliament of Canada (s.91[1]). In addition, all earlier proposals had assumed that amendments which concern Parliament and one or some provinces *only* may be achieved by legislative action of the concerned parties. [2] s. = section; h. = subsection. [3] Delegation: the transfer of powers between, and by mutual consent of, two levels of government.

has there been a formula with no protection for each province on at least some parts of the list of provincial powers. Even during the Depression, when the need for national solutions to social and economic distress led to demands for transferring provincial powers to Ottawa, many parts of section 92 required unanimous consent of the provinces for changes. Even constitutional changes in the vital area of property and civil rights (section 92, head 13) and local matters (section 92, head 16), which might be made without unanimity, could still be evaded by a province "opting out."

What is striking in the variation of the pattern is the increase in the areas requiring unanimity during the postwar period of federal pre-eminence. In 1950, to combat centralizing pressures, Ontario and Quebec demanded that the whole division of powers be entrenched; nothing could be changed without unanimous consent. This inflexibility made it highly unlikely that Ottawa would gain any powers from the provinces other than the bare minimum acceptable to all provinces. Despite vigorous opposition from Saskatchewan (where a CCF government placed a high priority on national social security programs), that blanket protection for the provinces continued through part of the 1960s, with the special provisions for delegation offering the only flexibility. Yet in 1964 even so security-conscious a formula as Fulton-Favreau, which gave every province a veto over any changes in the division of powers, was found unacceptable by Quebec premier Jean Lesage. By then, with the "Quiet Revolution" underway, the formula appeared to threaten Quebec's own aspirations.

After it took power in 1960, Lesage's new, confident administration in Quebec reversed the defensive nationalist policies of its predecessors and began to demand more powers for Quebec under a more flexible amendment procedure. In this campaign of national self-awakening, Quebecers found an understanding ally in the province of Ontario. Ontario shared Quebec's concerns over earlier federal intrusions into provincial jurisdictions, and it fully sympathized with that province's determination to develop provincial power. Ontario had already begun to build up administrative power and expertise to rival Ottawa's and it strongly resented federal pretensions to pre-eminence. Since it was axiomatic that Ontario with its vast population could not occupy a status inferior to that of Quebec, Ontario was virtually carried along with Quebec's demands for preferred status. The radical new formula which Prime Minister Trudeau offered in 1971 met these concerns, while at the same time it made changes wanted by the federal government easier to achieve.

In Trudeau's so-called Victoria formula, the protections of unanimity for all provinces were removed in exchange for a permanent veto for Quebec and Ontario. For the first time the inequality of provinces was openly declared as a guiding principle in the formula. Under the new arrangement, Quebec and Ontario could secure their constitutional objectives even with half of the provinces in the Atlantic region and the West in opposition. But provincial authority could be transferred to the federal level in crucial natural resource fields, such as control and ownership of oil and gas, without the agreement of Alberta, for example. Though this formula, so heavily weighted in favour of Central Canada, nearly passed in 1971 (Quebec finally pulled out feeling it had not won enough power over "social policy" in return for its agreement to patriation), by 1976 it was unacceptable to Alberta, British Columbia and others.

The play of political interest and the distrust it generated is evident in all the formulae forged over the years. Three interrelated dimensions of conflict cut across the deliberations: the weaker provinces' hostility toward Central Canada; the central provinces' rivalry with the federal government; and the linguistic division between Quebec and the other provinces. In the end, most players simply preferred the safety of the British connection to the uncertain dangers of a final Canadian constitutional marriage.

But the impasse on procedure did not bring the substance of constitutional change to a standstill. It was still possible to change the legislative division of powers by common agreement of the governments. In fact, during this period there were two major transfers of provincial authority to the federal government: unemployment insurance in 1940 and old age pensions in 1950. In addition, either level of government had the power to change its own constitutional area: section 92(1) of the BNA Act gave the provinces the power to amend matters in their own exclusive jurisdiction except for the office of lieutenant governor, and the British North America Act (Number 2), passed in 1949, enabled Parliament to alter its exclusive areas (section 91[1]). Moreover, the constitution still permitted special changes of particular importance to one or more provinces but not to all. The admission of Newfoundland into the union in 1949 by agreement of that province and Parliament was a good example of the flexibility that existed despite federal-provincial deadlock on a general amending procedure.

## The Founding Peoples and a Charter of Rights

Beginning in the 1960s, after the postwar period of federal leadership, an explosive growth of province-building especially in Quebec and Ontario shifted the constitutional balance of power toward the provinces. Ontario was disturbed about being forced into national programs such as medicare and preferred instead to enlarge its own capacity. Quebec demanded a restructuring of the Canadian state so that it reflected the duality of the two peoples of Canada and gave Quebecers plenty of elbow room to be "masters in their own house."

Quebecers demanded that the Quebec state strengthen French language and culture, modernize the educational system, take a more decisive role in the planning and direction of the economy, which traditionally (and especially during the long reactionary rule of Premier Maurice Duplessis) had been left largely to anglophones, and secure a better deal for Quebec either within or if necessary outside the federal system. These demands came from francophones who increasingly saw themselves as Québécois rather than French Canadians, and they reflected a new national awakening in the province. Quebecers demanded a status worthy of a distinct people, a "nation" occupying a "homeland" with as yet an imperfect means to express itself. Quebec francophones rapidly came to accept these values and the resulting need to expand Quebec's constitutional powers. At the same time, many Quebecers sought explicit recognition of the role of the French fact in the Canadian state, which apart from Quebec had for so long been entirely founded on English Canadian supremacy.

Two branches of Quebec's new post-Duplessis elite

expressed these feelings of national awakening in diametrically opposed strategies. One branch, which gravitated toward the "Quebec as homeland" option, was a fusion of separatist and radical nationalist groups that splintered off from the moderate nationalism fostered by Liberal Premier Jean Lesage and moved toward the goal of Quebec independence. This movement emerged as a powerful political force with the founding of the Parti Québécois in 1968 under the leadership of René Lévesque, a former minister in the Lesage cabinet. The other branch of the Quebec elite, under the leadership of Pierre Elliott Trudeau, expressed Quebec's national resurgence in a concerted effort to restructure *Canada as the homeland* for *all* francophones. The options then became renewed federalism versus separatism, Canada or Quebec as homeland. This struggle within Quebec's francophone elite has dominated Canada's constitutional politics for the past two decades.

Quebec's "Quiet Revolution" rocked the Ottawa establishment. In 1965, in part as a response to Quebec's aspirations, Prime Minister Lester Pearson's Liberal government passed the Established Programs Act, permitting provinces to opt out of certain shared-cost national programs and to receive financial compensation. Since the areas in which compensation were provided, such as medical and social assistance plans, were under provincial jurisdiction in any case, it seemed both fair and appropriate to do so. But because only Quebec took advantage of the offer and set up its own programs, the province acquired a *de facto* "special status" which troubled Quebec federalists like Trudeau. In a related gesture of accommodation, Ottawa proceeded to add more Quebecers to the federal civil service, and to commission and then act on the Report on Bilingualism and Biculturalism.

Yet the steady advance of separatist sentiment in Quebec signalled an emerging crisis for Canada. The rise of the Front de Libération du Québec and the increasing political terrorism in the province, which culminated in the October Crisis of 1970, made the legitimate movement for independence seem more menacing. It was natural for federalists in English-speaking Canada and Quebec to see major constitutional reform as an appropriate response to this threat. Prodded by Ontario's Confederation of Tomorrow Conference in 1967, the Pearson government started the first of a series of federal-provincial constitutional conferences in February 1968. The leader of the federal strategy against separatism and nationalism in Quebec was already effectively Pierre Elliott Trudeau, then Pearson's minister of justice. Under his direction, a plan was prepared for enshrining and popularizing the "homeland Canada" option.

The broad thrust of federal political strategy depended on patriating the constitution and entrenching a charter of rights which would symbolize the common political values of all Canadians and which would secure the French fact from coast to coast. This linking of civil liberties with the protection of French language rights was a politically artful response to the rise of separatism. For English Canada, a rights charter defused anglophone backlash against French power such as bedevilled the Official Languages Act, a federal statute enacted in 1968; within Quebec it promised to undercut the notion that Quebec was the only home for francophones. Presented as a question of "rights," this strategy for national unity pitted the rhetorical power of "freedom" against the Sirens' call of Quebec nationalism.

But the nation-building potential of a charter of rights could be expected to go well beyond symbolism and rhetoric. As careful students of American constitutional developments have long recognized, a rights charter as interpreted by a pro-federal Supreme Court can declare and enforce common values and practices in an otherwise diverse federation. In fact, no other national institution might attempt to do so with a surer authority than a court under the venerable mantle of constitutional law. There was therefore more than a hint of covert war against the excesses of Quebec nationalism and regionalism in Trudeau's proposal for unified values under a charter of rights.

Needless to say, the political strategy was disguised with simple talk of "people's rights." In fact, the whole federal plan was sold as a "people's package," which did not directly concern governments or powerfully affect the balance of federal-provincial relations. Although technically an entrenched charter would subtract legislative power from each level of the federation (though not necessarily equally), the power to pronounce on human rights would by the charter be transferred to the federally appointed Supreme Court of Canada. Under these conditions, enforcement of the people's charter might unify the country around individual rights, challenge the moral primacy of Canada's regional communities and resolve some of the chronic historical grievances of the French- and English-speaking peoples.

Naturally, as the chief custodians of regionalism, the provinces were not enthusiastic about an entrenched national charter. But its public appeal was difficult to resist. After a period of inconclusive negotiations, a much reduced charter was agreed to by first ministers at Victoria, in June 1971.

In addition to the amending formula discussed earlier, the Victoria Charter provided for the entrenchment of certain fundamental rights — freedom of thought, conscience and religion; freedom of opinion and expression; freedom of peaceful assembly and association — subject to a broad override. These freedoms could be limited "in the interests of public safety, order, health or morals, of national security, or of the rights and freedoms of others." Political rights were reaffirmed in that there could be no discrimination against a citizen's political rights on grounds of "national origin, colour, religion or sex." In the key area of linguistic rights, the Trudeau government gave way to provincial opposition over the entrenchment of minority language educational rights and legal and equality rights in return for provincial agreement to extend the protection of the French language in political and legal institutions. In the charter, French was declared an official language which could be used in every provincial legislature but Saskatchewan, Alberta and British Columbia; both official languages would prevail in the courts of Quebec, New Brunswick and Newfoundland; all provincial statutes were to be published in both languages; French might be used in communication with provincial governments in Ontario, Quebec, New Brunswick, Prince Edward Island and Newfoundland; and any extensions of these rights by a province could not later be revoked except by constitutional amendment. In terms of the earlier constitution and history of Canada, these initiatives by the English-speaking provinces were a dramatic turnaround, and a logical step from the 1968 Official Languages Act.

In return, Ottawa promised to consult provinces on appointments to the Supreme Court, to provide for a

majority of Supreme Court justices trained in civil
law, to repeal its power to reserve and disallow legislation passed by the provinces, and to concede provincial supremacy in certain areas of social policy like
family, youth and occupational allowances. Since
social policy was mostly under provincial jurisdiction,
in effect Ottawa had to renounce the right to initiate
national programs in these areas without consultation
and to leave room for provinces to pursue their own
programs. Evidently the concessions were not regarded as sufficient in Quebec, however, for no sooner
had Premier Robert Bourassa returned home from
Victoria than he was subjected to intense pressure to
back out of the provisional agreement. When the
Quebec premier caved in, he scuttled the prospects for
constitutional talks for the next few years.

Although discussion of the issue continued through
public meetings sponsored by the Special Joint Committee of the Senate and House of Commons on the
Constitution of Canada, it was not until 1974 that
Prime Minister Trudeau again broached the subject of
an amending formula. After getting a lukewarm response from the provinces, Trudeau began to drop the
first of many hints that Ottawa might act unilaterally if
consensus could not be achieved at least on patriation,
an amending formula and a charter of rights. As for
the provinces, most key players demanded increased
provincial powers as part of any overall settlement.
Although discussions proceeded in 1975 and 1976, the
prospects for agreement were not encouraging.

The 1976 election of the Parti Québécois, which
promised good government and a referendum on
"sovereignty-association," helped set the stage for a
resolution of the constitutional question. For the first
time the two hostile francophone elites confronted one

another from their respective bunkers in Quebec City and Ottawa. Over the next four years a propaganda war was waged for the hearts and minds of Quebecers with the future of Quebec and Canada in the balance. The debate covered familiar ground: the costs and benefits of federalism and separatism; federalism versus separatism as a protector of Quebec's distinctive language and culture; Trudeau's individual and minority rights versus Lévesque's "tribal" nationalism; Quebec or Canada as homeland. Although Claude Ryan, the former influential newspaper publisher who replaced Bourassa as leader of the Liberal party in Quebec, formally carried the banner of battle within the province, especially as the May 1980 referendum date approached, it was always Trudeau and Lévesque who captured the imagination of Quebecers. Each stood as a powerful symbol of Quebecers' split loyalties toward a new Canada and a new Quebec.

Since maintenance of the status quo was never an option, it was expected that serious constitutional change would result from this struggle, no matter who won. The 1976 separatist victory had shocked English-speaking Canada out of its complacency. Appeals to Quebecers to stay in the union poured in from all parts of Canada. Never before had Canadians been so moved to defend the ideal of a federal union or so ready to admit the shortcomings of their Confederation. This unity movement, blessed and supported by the federal government, reached its high point immediately prior to the May 1980 referendum. Popular expressions of the movement included sentimental vehicles such as the "people-to-people" petition, which pleaded with Quebecers to stay in Canada, while more enterprising groups set to work revamping the British North America Act. Much of this amateur constitution making was naïve, if well motivated. Over the next few years, there were enough constitutional proposals floating about to confound specialists, let alone the general public. But the process of public participation in constitutional renewal mattered more than the product; the groundwork was being laid for public acceptance and expectation of constitutional change.

While the federal government abetted the movement by sending on tour the Pepin-Robarts Task Force on Canadian Unity, many provinces — especially British Columbia and Ontario — and Quebec's Liberal Party under Claude Ryan prepared reports on several aspects of constitutional reform. These initiatives turned up a longer list of grievances, more proposals and even more hope for comprehensive change.

Surprisingly, however, this public celebration of federalism before the dark spectre of a separatist Quebec did not lead the provincial governments of English Canada to rally around Ottawa. Although Trudeau strengthened his bargaining hand over linguistic rights, especially after the passage in 1976 of Quebec's Bill 101, the language bill declaring Quebec unilingual, he could not translate public fears over separatism into federal pre-eminence. Tough bargaining over the constitution went on as usual. Nor did separatism give Quebec more muscle with other governments. Quebecers were later to learn that having installed the separatists in power with no separatist mandate, they had weakened their province's bargaining power in the constitutional talks.

## Regionalism and the Rise of the West

The second, but hardly noticed event which prepared

the way for Canada's new constitution was the emergence of a unified constitutional interest in the Western provinces. After the Organization of Petroleum Exporting Countries' cartel brought about a spectacular rise in oil and gas prices beginning in 1973, the politics of energy accentuated Western discontent. Alberta, British Columbia and Saskatchewan, the resource-rich provinces, were thrust into the front ranks of political and constitutional discussions. The premiers of these provinces began to plan joint initiatives, and for the first time since Confederation a regional bloc emerged with the power to rival Ontario and Quebec.

Under Western leadership, the politics of regionalism was given new momentum and legitimacy. The Atlantic and Western regions had always protested the domination of the Canadian state and economy by Central Canada, but their demands for change became pressing as the prospects of wealth from oil and gas appeared to give at least some of the provinces in these regions an equal chance to prosper. But federal policy over these natural resources seemed to threaten the development of these regions. Apart from federal insistence on holding control over offshore resources, the chief struggle took place over the price for oil and gas in Canada, which Ottawa kept at artificially low levels. (Electrical energy from Central Canada was not treated in a similar manner.) An aggravating factor was Ottawa's choice of Sarnia, Ontario, as the location of a major petrochemical refinery, an industry Alberta was trying to foster. In addition, Ottawa consistently lowered the potential revenues for the West from their resources by imposing a variety of tax measures, including export surcharge taxes. When Saskatchewan sought to maximize the benefits it received from its resources by enacting measures to ration potash (to restrict supply and indirectly fix export prices), and to tax excess profits on oil, Ottawa sided with the private companies involved in a successful constitutional challenge to the resource powers of the provinces in 1974. All of these actions pushed the producing provinces into a united regional bloc which demanded that Ottawa stop exploiting Western resoures for the benefit of Central Canada and the Liberals' electoral base there.

Such a political and constitutional challenge was also attractive to the provinces in Eastern Canada. Not only did they share the resentment over Central Canadian dominance, they also anticipated a better economic future. Newfoundland and Nova Scotia sympathized with Western Canadian claims and sought to enlist Western support in their bid for control and development of offshore resources. In this respect, the economics of regionalism were certainly powerful enough to offset any timidity arising from the East's "have-not" status.

But the rise of regionalism was not just a matter of jurisdictional disputes. Canada was already beginning to feel the effects of a powerful shift in economic and political power away from Central Canada. The West was challenging the historic model of Canada with its growing cities and wealth. The state of Western provincial finances and investment funds was healthier than those of Quebec or Ontario, both of which were experiencing a severe weakening of their manufacturing base. Thus when the provinces from the Western and Atlantic regions demanded a new deal from Canada, they did so not primarily out of historic grievances but because contemporary realities demanded that Canada's emerging patterns of power be recognized.

With these pressures, the agenda for constitutional change expanded beyond the federally sponsored "people's package" to include two major provincial concerns. The first was the renegotiation of the division of powers to increase the provinces' powers, especially over offshore and onshore natural resources and communications (telephone and broadcasting systems). Such authority in provincial capitals would strengthen local economic and cultural development and place Canadians' regional loyalties on a stronger footing. In addition, under consideration were proposals to give control over family law matters such as marriage and divorce to the provinces, to give provinces some powers over the fisheries, and to enshrine the principle of equalization payments to have-not provinces in the constitution. The second major concern was to "federalize" the central institutions in Ottawa, especially the Senate and Supreme Court, so that their membership and direction would better reflect distinct provincial interests and needs. The fathers of Confederation had intended the Senate to perform this function, but it had never done so. Instead the Senate had the reputation of a rest home for retired politicians who rarely defied the House of Commons. The Supreme Court, whose members were also exclusively appointed by Ottawa, was similarly suspected of having a pro-federal bias. By permitting a stronger role for provincial governments in shaping these institutions, it was hoped that regional alienation from Ottawa would decline.

With Quebec in the hands of the separatists and regional demands becoming stronger, Trudeau felt that the time for federal action was approaching. Discouraged with the pace of negotiations, he unveiled in 1978 a two-phase process of reform and constitutional change in Bill C-60. Phase one (deadline, July 1, 1979) would complete the updating of the British North America Act in federal areas of jurisdiction; phase two (deadline, July 1, 1981 — the fiftieth anniversary of the Statute of Westminster) would complete the process in the thorny area of federal-provincial powers. Although phase one would be undertaken with as much provincial consultation as possible, the federal government maintained that all the changes fell directly within its own jurisdiction and that they therefore could be implemented unilaterally under section 91 (1). The federal plan for phase one was to entrench a preamble stating the aims of the Canadian federation subscribed to by Parliament, to entrench a Canadian charter of human rights and freedoms in federal areas of jurisdiction only, to entrench the Supreme Court of Canada and change its composition, and to reform the Senate.

That strategy ended in disaster. Not only did Parliament fail to meet its deadline, but, under pressure from the opposition and from provincial premiers, the government referred the question of its unilateral right to amend the Senate to the Supreme Court. It lost. The court found that provincial consent was necessary to such a restructuring. As an essentially federal institution, the Senate could not be considered a subject purely within the concern of a single level of government.

Meanwhile, for Ottawa, life at the bargaining table was getting no easier. The combination of powerful Western provinces and Quebec, together with more aggressive regional pressures from Atlantic Canada, especially Newfoundland, was not easy to resist. The demands on federal powers in many areas, from the fisheries to international relations, had never been greater nor their implications more serious for the federation as a whole. While signalling a willingness to compromise, the federal government attempted to limit the extent of the concessions as much as possible and to secure in return an agreement on linguistic rights. Trudeau was determined to have action "before the electors of Quebec are called upon ... to choose between political independence on the one hand, and on the other, the preservation of a status quo which federal and provincial governments have proved incapable of changing despite 51 years of effort."

By February 1979 the federal government appeared ready to accept the demands of the West over natural resources, even if other issues still remained unresolved. However, the Liberal agenda was put into limbo by the defeat of Trudeau's government on May 22, 1979, and the formation of a Conservative minority government under Joe Clark. The Clark government's idea of Canada as a federal state was much closer to regionalism. Clark's theme of Canada as a "community of communities" was sweet music to the premiers' ears, especially when it promised transfers of powers on offshore jurisdiction to the provinces. It looked as though federal-provincial conflict was about to be toned down and that Trudeau and his plans would become mere footnotes in the history of failure over the constitution. But the Clark government's inexperience turned events around. Not seven months later, its first budget was repudiated in the House of Commons on the eve of Trudeau's would-be political retirement. The country was immediately forced into an election which pre-campaign polls suggested would be won by the Liberal party under Trudeau. He and his lieutenants, especially cabinet veteran Allan MacEachen, reversed the earlier Liberal defeat and on election night, February 18, 1980, a triumphant Trudeau was returned with a majority just in time to take on his old separatist enemies in the May 1980 referendum.

As it turned out, the federal campaign against separatism had to be waged without any constitutional renewal. The only positive alternative which the federalists inside and outside of Quebec offered was the *promise* of significant change. That promise was made by Quebec Liberal leader Claude Ryan, but more particularly by Prime Minister Trudeau and virtually all of the provincial premiers. In the end Quebecers decided to deny Lévesque the mandate to negotiate sovereignty-association for which he had campaigned so hard. The vote was not overwhelming, however, since 40.5 per cent of the electorate were ready to choose the separatist route. It was also not an absolute vote of approval for federalism, but one conditional upon significant reform. If the fight for a federal union — for one and not two Canadas — were to succeed, the onus would now be upon the winners to give form to their rhetoric at the constitutional negotiating table.

# 2
# Option 1: Negotiation with the Provinces

Prime Minister Trudeau lost no time in pressing home his advantage in the wake of the PQ referendum: after sending his constitutional lieutenant and justice minister, Jean Chrétien, on a whirlwind tour of provincial capitals, he summoned the premiers to a First Ministers' Conference in Ottawa on June 9, 1980.

To the federal Liberals, constitutional renewal meant resolving the "Quebec problem" without fanning the flames of regionalism. They were prepared to offer certain concessions to the provinces (though preferably less than what circumstances had forced them to agree to in February 1979) in return for securing linguistic justice for the two founding peoples. As usual, the Liberal conception of such a settlement between English- and French-speaking Canadians was the entrenchment of bilingualism and of the educational rights of official linguistic minorities all across the country. This program for national unity and renewal was contained within the "people's

package" of human rights and freedoms, together
with patriation of the Canadian constitution. Although events would later show that the federal
Liberals were ready to compromise on almost all the
general human rights and freedoms in the package —
until left with a weak charter of rights that made a
mockery of legal protection of civil liberties — they
were not willing to give up the linguistic core of their
strategy.

The link between this plan for federal renewal and
the political revival of Pierre Elliott Trudeau was
obvious. After being snatched from would-be retirement, delivered with an election victory and then permitted to preside as prime minister over a federalist
win in the Quebec referendum, Trudeau must have
found events more than a little fateful. In politics, such
a resurrection could not but be portentous. Even
before the June meeting, Trudeau had determined
that, with or without the premiers, the government
would act swiftly to implement *at least* that constitutional package.

But the post-referendum outlook of most provinces
was quite different from Trudeau's. The federalist
victory reduced concern over national unity as it
affected linguistic matters and encouraged a com-
placent attitude toward the "Quebec problem,"
especially since the Parti Québécois was now thought
to be a lame duck government. The premiers, boast-
ing not a single Liberal among them, mostly looked
to constitutional renewal for solutions to their own
regional grievances and could not support the political timetable of a national government so heavily
dominated by Ontario interests and anti-separatist
Quebecers.

In between these two colliding views sat a reluctant player. The PQ government, its sovereignty-association proposal rejected, was in the awkward position of complying with the federalist option against which it had so recently campaigned. Not only was Lévesque's government expected to negotiate *within* the Canadian federation, but to do so gracefully. Under no circumstances, therefore, would Quebec permit itself to be isolated on any item during the negotiation process. Since the regional conception of a federal state suited it far better than Trudeau's idea of Canada, it was easy enough for Quebec to align itself with the discontented blocs of provinces without taking a strong leadership role and then to await the outcome. If the talks failed, it would be vital to show Quebec's ongoing cooperation in the negotiations and to demonstrate that the process necessarily betrayed Quebec's deepest interests. If the federalists were not to play into the hands of the separatists, an accommodation would be required.

But events on June 9 did not suggest that such a bargain would be likely. A statement of constitutional principles that would have affirmed federalism and the status of the French and English languages was proposed by Trudeau and rejected by the premiers. They preferred instead to leave these broad issues to be defined during the summer's negotiations. Moreover, the agreed agenda of twelve items was a pot-pourri of federal and provincial interests with no clear priorities or linkages made to competing conceptions of the country. To resolve all twelve topics — natural resources, communications, the Senate and Supreme Court, family law, fisheries, offshore jurisdiction, equalization, a charter of rights and amending for-

mula, powers over the economy, and a preamble —
within the strict three-month timetable (June 9 –
September 8) imposed by Trudeau was a tall order.

Since there was no grappling with the inherently
contradictory agendas advanced by regional and
national actors, nor with the relative priorities or
possible compromises within them, the struggle to
define the shape of Canada would have to be fought
out on every agenda item and any concessions left to
be settled on an *ad hoc* basis. The three "packages"
into which the agenda could be divided were too complicated to become the basis of federal-provincial
trade-offs even if the negotiations had been structured
to produce such a result.

These packages consisted of the "people's package"
desired by Ottawa, which included patriation (with the
usual federal-provincial dispute over an amending
formula), the Charter of Rights, and a new constitutional preamble; an "institutions package" to include
a new Senate and a new Supreme Court, largely supported by both levels of government but of special
interest to the provinces; and a "powers package" of
agenda items of which all but "powers over the
economy" were provincial concerns. The first was
essentially the federal nation-building plan which
clashed with the ambitions of the PQ and of the
regional interests of other actors. As a bloc of constitutional demands it could not be simply exchanged
for the powers package since there were too many
objectionable features in it. From the point of view of
the federal government, the powers package could not
be accepted as a bloc since only *some* of the provincial
demands were seriously negotiable. Moreover virtually every item in the powers package invited a dispute between the parties over the merits of national

and regional perspectives. Even the institutions package was riddled with the same tensions.

Given the unwieldiness of the packages, progress toward an acceptable common ground depended heavily on flexibility by the key players, especially over resource topics and the Charter of Rights. The importance of these issues was reflected in the choice of the co-chairmen of the Continuing Committee of Ministers on the Constitution. Justice Minister Jean Chrétien symbolized the stake the federal Quebec elite put in securing their referendum victory through an entrenched national charter; Roy Romanow, attorney general of Saskatchewan, symbolized the now dominant, resource-conscious Western leadership among the provinces. If an agreement were to emerge, these interests had to come to terms.

But, no such entente developed. Instead, the provinces generally worked toward compromise and consensus *among themselves* on most agenda matters to foil any federal use of "divide and rule" tactics, and they were determined not to give ground over the key federal interest, the charter. In building an interprovincial common front, this strategy worked remarkably well. Despite divergent regional interests, the West and most of the East, including Quebec, joined forces in a common front on most agenda items, thus isolating Ottawa and its most consistent ally, Ontario.

Although Ontario had been one of the first to show the other provinces the rudiments of province building with its own administrative growth and development planning, it did not wish to see its fellow provinces use their new bureaucratic expertise to upset Ontario's comfortable position in Confederation. Hence, Ontario backed Ottawa in its confrontation with the Parti Québécois and generally accepted federal plans for constitutional extension of minority language educational rights and for a charter of rights (provided, of course, that Ontario itself was not legally compelled to bear the financial and political costs of becoming a bilingual province). Ontario took a similarly self-interested stance when it sided with Ottawa in its showdown with Alberta over energy pricing. As the chief beneficiary of the national economy policy for many generations, Ontario was also disturbed at obstructions to the national market which provincial or regional preferential policies for hiring and buying presented. Ontario accordingly backed Ottawa's demands for stronger national control over the economy. Such a record compromised Ontario's ability to play its preferred role as "honest broker" between the contending interests.

The federal government played its hand cagily. On one side, it took a tough negotiating posture, especially over resource topics and the economy; on the other, it refused to commit itself firmly on subjects like communications, the Senate or the Supreme Court. In fact, Ottawa offered the provinces *less* than what it had been prepared to give in the February 1979 talks. On natural resources, it pulled back from its offer to give provinces power over interprovincial trade in natural resources except in situations of "compelling national interest" and it refused to budge from its position that provincial power should not extend to international trade in these resources. In addition to withdrawing some earlier offers, Ottawa brought forward the entirely new "powers over the economy," an item designed to counteract any concessions it might make to the producing provinces. To strengthen federal control over the economy and bar special provincial protectionist measures, such as "locals first" labour policies and restrictive property laws, Ottawa demanded more powers over trade and commerce, a strengthened section 121 which would prohibit protectionist barriers to the economic union and an entrenchment of mobility rights, which would entitle Canadians to move to another province, gain employment and buy property there.

The other side of the federal game plan consisted of offering partial concessions to the provinces and, where convenient, in expressing benign non-commitment. Although federal planners had made provision for further compromises if provinces met their vital demands, there was no question that Ottawa was playing hard ball in anticipation of a break in provincial resistance to the charter. It never came.

In fact the provinces had been brought to near or complete unanimity on the principle of a charter at least twice in the prior decade: first with the Victoria Charter, and recently, in the February 1979 negotiations. By the time of the summer 1980 negotiations, however, the positions of most provinces — especially those in Western Canada — had stiffened considerably. With the separatists defeated in the referendum, the provinces began to listen more and more to Manitoba's arguments that the charter was not compatible with parliamentary democracy and that it would cause a massive shift of power from legislatures to courts. Such a transfer would in their view seriously disrupt provincial ambitions for regional development. Some sections of the proposed charter, especially mobility rights, struck hard at provincial power to foster economic development, as did the federal proposal for a national economic union. There was no question that many parts of the charter would limit the legislative authority of provinces who, after all, had exclusive authority over "property and civil rights." What made the whole question dangerous was that it was impossible to judge just how far the charter might limit provincial powers.

But provincial concerns were not confined to a defence of the provinces' constitutional turf; often they were honest reactions to the administrative head-aches, cost or policy implications of a charter. For example, the right of witnesses in criminal and penal proceedings to give evidence either in French or English placed a heavy financial and administrative burden on the provinces. The right to equality ap-peared to limit the ability of the provinces to apply affirmative action programs, while the right to hold property threatened the land control measures of Prince Edward Island and Saskatchewan. Mobility rights appeared to deprive have-not provinces of the power to defend their residents with job preferences, and all provinces of the power to regulate professional groups within the province.

If the provincial governments were unhappy with many of the specific provisions as well as the principle of a charter, the federal Liberals were most disap-pointed over the lack of support for their linguistic strategy. Only four provinces supported the entrench-ment of minority language educational rights, with most siding with the Parti Québécois on the issue.

By the time the Continuing Committee of Ministers on the Constitution met again in Ottawa in August just prior to the First Ministers' Conference, many of the provinces' objections to the charter had been con-sidered by the federal government and minor adjust-ments made. The only major changes were the eli-mination of property rights from the package, the exception of affirmative action programs from the equality rights provision, the promise that courts would not necessarily exclude improperly obtained evidence, and the elimination of the right of witnesses in criminal and penal proceedings to give evidence in either English or French. Most provinces, however, continued to propose more serious changes or deletions in an attempt to gut the charter. After demanding the deletion of many sections, including equality and mobility rights, and the emasculation of most of the legal rights, the provinces proposed that the charter be scrapped in favour of strengthening the 1960 Canadian Bill of Rights. Federal officials brushed off this proposal as inadequate since it would apply only at the federal level, it would ignore language rights, and it would not guarantee basic common rights throughout Canada.

The federal and provincial positions had now become more polarized over the charter than they had ever been. Only New Brunswick, Ontario and Newfoundland even accepted the principle of an entrenched Charter. The Liberal spirit of nation building was being spurned by provincial elites, while federal Liberals came to regard regionalism and province building as but "separatism by another name". And yet, negotiations over many agenda items other than the charter were progressing remarkably well. As Table 2 shows, on family law, equalization, patriation, the Senate and the Supreme Court there was, sometimes in the absence of a clear federal position, substantial agreement on changes. On all other fronts, there were still important differences, though none so great that an acceptable deal could not have been hammered out provided the provinces supported the

*Table 2*

## CONSTITUTIONAL DISCUSSIONS BY AGENDA ITEM, SEPTEMBER 11, 1980

| Topics | Agreed Matters[1] | Continuing Differences |
|---|---|---|
| Natural Resources | • recognize provincial ownership and management of non-renewable resources, forestry and electrical energy<br><br>• grant provinces power over interprovincial trade in resources, subject to federal paramountcy[2]<br><br>• grant provinces power to apply indirect taxes on resources provided they do not discriminate against citizens of other provinces | • federal side refused to do away with declaratory power[3] over natural resources<br><br>• federal side refused to grant power over international trade in these resources<br><br>• federal side refused February 1979 best-efforts draft giving provinces paramountcy over trade in resources except when there is "a compelling national interest" |
| Communications | • grant provinces power over intraprovincial telephone systems<br><br>• provincial power to license, set rates, and regulate cable intraprovincially | • federal side refused provincial proposal to establish concurrency[4] with provincial paramountcy on everything but frequency allocation and management, networks extending over four or more provinces |

|  |  | • foreign broadcasting, satellites, aeronautical communications, radio-navigation, defence, or emergencies |
| --- | --- | --- |
| Senate | • provinces to be better and directly represented | • number and powers of federal appointees in Senate<br>• provincial representation<br>• status and powers of a possible council of the provinces as part of the new Senate, with veto powers over certain federal decisions affecting the provinces<br>• the future of the Senate as a house of general legislative review |
| Fisheries | • province to gain right to consultation and administrative input<br>• provinces to gain almost all control over inland fisheries | • seven provinces, led by Newfoundland, wanted concurrent jurisdiction with federal paramountcy only on international fishing, conservation and limits on total allowable catch |

*Table 2 continued*

| Topics | Agreed Matters[1] | Continuing Differences |
|---|---|---|
| Supreme Court | • entrench the Supreme Court in constitution<br>• direct right of provinces to pose reference questions to Supreme Court<br>• federal appointment of justices on consultation with provinces<br>• alternating civil and common law chief justice<br>• recognition of dualism[5] | • slight differences over number of justices; most wanting eleven, some nine<br>• differences on ratio of common law to civil law justices<br>• majority preferred to avoid Quebec's and Alberta's suggestion of a separate panel on constitutional questions<br>• how to resolve differences if federal and provincial attorneys general disagree on court appointments |
| Family Law | • concurrency over marriage and divorce with provincial paramountcy | • Manitoba and P.E.I. opposed, wishing national protection on this item, i.e., child custody orders |
| Offshore Resources | • provinces to get administrative arrangements for revenue sharing | • most provinces wanted offshore resources to be treated the same as |

|  |  |  |
|---|---|---|
|  | and input into policy planning | onshore resources, i.e., provincial ownership; Ottawa disagreed |
| Equalization | • entrench principle of equalization payments to have-not provinces<br>• provide for regular review of equalization mechanism | • slight differences over wording |
| Charter of Rights | | • substantial difference over principle<br>• some support from Ontario, N.B. and Newfoundland with Saskatchewan supporting only language provisions |
| Patriation and the Amending Formula | • support for patriation but provinces want agreement on division of powers first | • differences between N.B, Ontario, Saskatchewan, and federal side who wanted the Victoria formula and the others who supported the Alberta formula |

*Table 2 continued*

| Topics | Agreed Matters[1] | Continuing Differences |
|---|---|---|
| Powers Over the Economy | • all support the principle of economic union | • disagreement over whether union should be protected by court or political mechanism<br>• disagreement over entrenching mobility rights, strengthening federal powers over trade and commerce and over a strengthened section 121 which would ensure the free passage of goods, services and capital within Canada<br>• disagreement over qualifying clause which would permit affirmative action programs |
| Preamble | | • no clear agreement on wording or principle<br>• no agreement on including principle of self-determination for Quebec |

- concern over extent of encroach-
  ment of preamble on body of
  constitution

Notes:
[1] In this column are listed the *substantial* areas of agreement between the federal government and most provinces. Dissenters are noted in the right-hand column.
[2] "Paramountcy": Supremacy in the event of conflict in an area of joint jurisdiction.
[3] "Declaratory power": That the federal government can take over any "works" in a province that are declared by Parliament to be for the advantage of the country or of two or more provinces. In effect, this would permit Ottawa to assume ownership and control of any provincial project or industry.
[4] "Concurrency": That both levels of government may legislate in a given area.
[5] "Dualism": In this context, that the distinctiveness of Quebec's civil code required recognition by ensuring a guaranteed number of civil law justices on the Supreme Court.

core of the charter. A clear spirit of accommodation was beginning to develop in the tacit balancing off of resource ownership powers and the federal demand for powers over the economy.

On offshore resources, however, there was a chasm too big to bridge. Newfoundland's vigorous assertion that offshore resources be treated exactly as onshore resources are treated — in short a demand for provincial ownership — was supported by most provinces but got nowhere with the federal government. The federal side tried to placate the coastal provinces by offering them an administrative and revenue-sharing deal, but the item continued to be a stumbling block.

Alberta's new amending formula became a topic of considerable importance since it appeared to be the logical provincial alternative to the federally supported Victoria formula, with its protection for Ontario and Quebec. As outlined in Table 1, this formula for changing the constitution was based on two major principles: equality of provinces on constitutional change and the right of all provinces to "opt out" of certain classes of amendments directly affecting provincial rights and powers. Thus, Quebec and Ontario could still refuse the application of an amendment affecting their powers within their provinces, but there would be no permanent hegemony of *any* province over amendments that might be desired by many other governments. In this manner, Alberta hoped that the obnoxious feature of provincial inequality would begin to be expunged from Canadian federalism, and a general respect for provincial autonomy put in its place. By the end of the third week of meetings in July at Vancouver, a large provincial consensus had begun to develop around the Alberta proposal, which became known as the "Vancouver consensus."

Regional grievances also surfaced over the federal demand for increased powers over the economy. The Atlantic and Western provinces, suspicious of the free-market rhetoric of the federal and Ontario governments, argued that removal of all defensive measures undertaken mostly by have-not regions would not work toward the "equal benefit of all of Canada" but rather would exacerbate Canada's regional inequalities. Justice in the distribution of economic costs and benefits in Canada, they contended, was at least as important as any economist's abstract argument for economic efficiency in a pure economic union. They pointed out that the federal government itself recognized the same principle when it proposed to give job preferences to native peoples in Northern development.

Such were the typical cross-currents of interest and ideology which the negotiations had to bridge. It was clear that genuine renewal of Canadian federalism could not be completed without dealing with both the "Quebec problem" and Central Canadian domination of the federation. The failure of the talks stemmed from the inability of each side to recognize precisely the links between the federal and regional agendas and to make the necessary political sacrifices.

Hostile attitudes also limited the chances for success. Provincial leaders and officials doubted federal willingness to negotiate in good faith and were wary of manipulation by Ottawa mandarins like Michael Kirby and Jim Coutts. As secretary of the cabinet for federal-provincial relations, Kirby was deeply involved in masterminding what many premiers thought to be a cynical federal strategy. Coutts' influence as Trudeau's principal secretary was known to be that of a Liberal "backroom boy" par excellence. But the chief suspicion was reserved for Trudeau. His Machiavellian presence haunted the road-show constitutional conference throughout the summer and contributed in no small part to provincial savaging of the charter.

The federal view of the provinces was hardly more flattering. While the Parti Québécois government had long been dismissed as "tribal," Western and Atlantic regionalism was now diagnosed as but a milder form of the same disease. In the 1980 election, Trudeau had lectured the West on the need for sharing and had treated Newfoundland's claims over the offshore as hardly more than parochial greed. Even Premier Davis, who could usually be charitably exempted from the brush of provincialism, was damned for toadying to the prejudices of backwater Ontario on linguistic matters. These attitudes dampened federal interest in the negotiations and they certainly prepared and appeared to justify plans for unilateral action.

The strategic approaches of the players also undermined the negotiations. The provinces' attempt to build up a consensus on agenda issues, with the leadership on each topic usually reserved for the province (or provinces) with the most at stake, was an unfruitful course of action. It tended to blur serious differences between the provinces in order to get at best a tenuous consensus; it encouraged the development of an "all-or-nothing" attitude to the whole package of constitutional reform; it left the provincial consensus on each item to be defined by the provincial "leader" with the most far-reaching demands on federal powers; and it put the whole context of negotiations into a bilateral instead of multilateral framework. Thus Newfoundland defined for most provinces the provincial consensus on offshore jurisdiction, Saskatchewan on natural resources, Alberta on the amending formula, British Columbia on the Senate, and Manitoba on the Charter of Rights. These tacit trade-offs between the provinces were acceptable since they gave each premier his pet project and since the total package strengthened regional and provincial power. But the federal government's priorities were necessarily left out in this strategy, a fact which brought unilateral action closer.

But if the provincial negotiating tactics overlooked the need to give ground on the federal government's central demand for an entrenched charter, the federal strategy, as disclosed in the so-called Kirby memorandum, simply underestimated provincial opposition to the charter. Rather than offering any practical suggestions to get around the fact that seven provinces disagreed with the principle of entrenchment, officials merely recommended concessions on wordings and offers of additional time to comply with the language rights section. This miscalculation was carried over into the total federal bargaining strategy, which assumed that "much of the resistance to the People's Package [the Charter of Rights, patriation, and the amending formula] has been to try to force the federal government to bargain within the Institutions and Powers Package." After mistakenly treating the charter issue as purely a provincial bargaining chip, the federal strategists went on to declare an "easy" strategy of partial concessions within the institutions and powers package which would lead the provinces "at the end of the day...to accept the People's Package."

The memorandum was, in that respect, a facile account of the issues and the flexibility possible over certain key agenda items. The government was led to believe that the separation of the "people's" from the "powers" package, the threats of unilateral action and the force of public opinion in the Gallup polls had "led to closer agreement on a Charter of Rights than there has been before." In fact, virtually all of the evidence pointed in the other direction. Within days of the memo's completion, there was a major struggle between the participants to persuade the public that the charter would alternately perfect or ruin Canada's traditions and future.

What may have made federal officials over-confident was the ever-present option of unilateral action, which had been actively entertained even before the negotiations had started. In the Kirby memorandum, federal officials urged their leaders to prepare the public for such an eventuality and also encouraged them to use unilateral action as a bargaining threat:

> In private, the provinces must be told that there is absolutely no question but that the federal government will proceed very quickly with *at least* all the elements of the People's Package and that it would therefore be to their advantage to bargain in good faith on the other issues so that they too will be relatively satisfied after the Conference. It should be made abundantly clear that on Powers and Institutions, the federal government expects *give* from the provinces as well as *take*.

Although the fallback to unilateral action was thought to be a reassuring alternative to a negotiated agreement, it was in fact a hazardous option. Yet officials returned to it after finally admitting in the last paragraph of the memorandum that "the probability of an agreement is not high."

When the first ministers arrived in Ottawa to open the conference on September 8, the seriousness of the differences over key items and the difficulties created by negotiating strategies were not fully appreciated. The first morning was devoted to an expression of the regional versus the national vision of Canada, despite the federal government's desire to avoid establishing fixed positions. As each province defended the regional theme, it inevitably took a harder line on its central constitutional preoccupations. The federal government then challenged the provincial complaints by maintaining that Canada was already the "most decentralized federation in the world," but argued that the provinces would none the less find the federal government flexible on many issues.

The public statement of positions, topic by topic, did not constitute negotiations. As the press kept a scorecard on who made the strongest public impact from day to day, the business of achieving an agreement slipped by. With television coverage of the talks and behind-the-scenes consultations with officials, the participants were under an enormous strain; "grandstanding" rather than a patient search for common ground was often the result. By the third day of the talks, September 10, when the federal and provincial governments reached a stand-off over the charter, the chances of bridging differences seemed to evaporate. In an eloquent debate over the "principle" of entrenchment, the participants managed to get themselves into hopelessly deadlocked positions.

The debate centred not on rights or linguistic justice but on the nature of the Canadian state, its institutions and its theory of government, and it left the participants further apart than ever. Manitoba's Conservative government had relentlessly fought an entrenched charter all along and Premier Sterling Lyon now set the tone for the debate. He began by charging that "entrenchment was contrary to our traditional and our successful Parliamentary government" and would move our system "towards that of a republican system." Quoting from a paper by G.P. Browne of Carleton University sent to all provincial delegations, Lyon declared that "such a transfer of legislative authority [from Parliaments to courts] would amount to a constitutional revolution entailing the relinquishment of the essential principle of Parliamentary democracy, the principle of Parliamentary supremacy."

By identifying the entrenchment of a charter of rights with the republican model, Lyon also established valuable lines of argument against the charter which were variously taken up by other opponents of the proposal. First, he argued, entrenchment of rights in the United States had not protected Americans any better than citizens in countries like Britain or Canada which had no entrenched rights; second, dubious court judgements on rights had left Americans collectively unable to deal effectively with issues like pornography, crime, the observance of religious and other community norms, and many other matters; third, the wisdom of forcing judges to legislate in the highly political and contentious field of human rights was in doubt; fourth, Canada's political culture and traditions were different from those of the United States and should be respected unless strong grounds could be advanced that revolutionary change would "be beneficial, not harmful"; and finally, rights should be defined and altered by legislatures elected by the public rather than by a few appointed "men, albeit learned in the law, who are not necessarily aware of everyday concerns of Canadians." Lyon finished by urging his colleagues "to retain our own heritage, and reject experiments with concepts foreign to our tradition."

Lyon's classically conservative attack on the charter was followed by that of Saskatchewan NDP Premier Allan Blakeney, which echoed the concern for community rights and democratic decision making over crucial social values such as capital punishment, obscenity and discrimination. "Canadians ought not to have taken away from them the fundamental right to participate in political choices, in particular they ought not to have eroded under the guise of advancing their freedoms their right to make important social choices and to participate in those decisions." To Blakeney, courts were forums giving "an advantage to the rich" and parliaments and legislatures "were less of an advantage to the rich." Therefore, in choosing which instrument was more likely to advance the rights of all, Blakeney wanted Canadians to lobby and not to litigate. Another undesirable consequence of using the courts to protect liberties, he said, was the promotion of "an adversarial society," such as in the United States.

The critics of the charter were advancing important political and philosophical objections, but they were undoubtedly weakest in their defence (explicit or implied) of Canada as a land of freedom where, as Lyon put it, "infringements of basic rights are rare." Trudeau attacked that assumption at the beginning of the discussion, although in a glaring omission he neglected to mention abuses arising from *his* government's invoking of the War Measures Act in 1970:

> It is within certainly our history and the memory of some of us that there have been laws denying basic rights, denying the franchise to Chinese citizens, Canadian citizens of British Columbia, for instance, abolishing the use of French in Manitoba where it had been guaranteed by the constitution or so the French thought. Stripping Japanese-Canadians of their citizenship by the federal government. Suppression of freedom of religion in Quebec. Restricting the rights of citizens to acquire property in some provinces, Prince Edward Island and Saskatchewan. Limiting the rights of citizens to seek employment from one province to another in Quebec and Newfoundland. Limiting the use of English in Quebec. The list is not enormous, but it can go on. . . .

Premier Hatfield of New Brunswick, who with Davis of Ontario was defending the charter, also declared that "all political jurisdictions are guilty of offending rights" and that none of them could therefore be trusted finally to protect and preserve them. He also reminded Premier Blakeney of the costs and difficulty of moving legislatures to undo violations that they may have committed. But Hatfield spoke to the centre of his concerns when he warned that he did not want any future government of New Brunswick to be able to declare the province unilingual, as the province of Quebec had done.

When Jean Chrétien spoke on behalf of the federal government, his central theme was the language provisions of the Charter of Rights. He admitted frankly that rectifying violations of minority education and language rights in both Quebec and English Canada was central to the government's purposes and that the charter was to "cure" these grievances forever. The general question of rights served as good politics for this strategy.

Defending civil rights was politically popular. It diverted Canadians away from their linguistic divisions and prejudices which the charter was to correct. Moreover, the entrenchment issue drew the public into the more abstract questions of parliamentary democracy and federalism. Calling the charter part of the "people's package" contributed to the general impression desired by the federal government. At the same time, its positive role in nation building recommended itself to federal strategists.

Quebec did not take the federal scolding on its treatment of its English-speaking minority lightly. Its premier declared that it had no lessons to learn on that score from any other jurisdiction in Canada and that rights in Quebec were being studiously and carefully protected. Lévesque further claimed that the charter sought to return the province to pre–Bill 101 days with the principle of free choice for French or English schools — a policy "absolutely contrary to the interests of Quebec." This charge drew out a federal rebuttal and yet more posturing by Quebec's political leaders.

It was a curiously muddled debate which pitted the strategy of constitutional entrenchment against separatism and the English tradition of parliamentary democracy in turn. Only the Quebec representatives understood and appreciated the irony of the confusions; most English-speaking federal and provincial politicians largely spoke past one another. Quebec successfully appealed to the other provinces in the language of regionalism against Trudeau's "authoritarian" federalism, while the other provinces interpreted the charter as an assault upon the English parliamentary tradition. It was a paradoxical fate for a federal initiative intended to reconcile Quebec to Canada and to rectify classic Canadian injustices.

After a sophistical attack upon the parliamentary supremacy argument, Trudeau in his concluding remarks came to the heart of the strategy being used to advance justice for linguistic minorities and its relationship to the preservation of the Canadian state. Quoting Lévesque that "one or two generations is all that remains to the [French-speaking] minorities" in English Canada and noting that even the English-speaking minority in Quebec was now lacking self-confidence, he drew out the stark contrasts of two futures for Canada:

> We have one province which is essentially French-speaking and the rest of the country which is essentially English-speaking, and that is almost what we have had for a long, long while. The question is: do we continue to reinforce this kind of Canada and, if so, there is no doubt in my mind, and I don't think in many of our minds, that that will end up in two Canadas. We have certainly the admission of the present government of Quebec, to whom the logic of that demographic reality led them to want to have Quebec opt out of Canada and become an independent political state, speaking French, tolerant to its minorities, with the rest of Canada speaking English. This is one direction in which we have been going and towards which we can continue to go.
>
> The other one, the other conception of Canada is a Canada which respects what Premier Blakeney I think very wisely called the bargain of Confederation.... That bargain of Canada, as we understand it, and I am talking "we," French-speaking Canadians, is that

anywhere in this country French will be respected and accepted as the right of a Canadian citizen.

Bilingualism, Trudeau argued, was important to Quebec and to the country despite the fears it generated in English-speaking Canada and despite the contemptuous dismissal of it in Quebec — especially by separatists who did not wish it to work. Cloaked under a mantle of human rights, this policy of national renewal was Trudeau's answer to Quebec nationalism. Such a program was not likely to be stopped by squabbles over Canada's parliamentary traditions or even by the niceties of Canada's conventions.

When the premiers gathered together for a breakfast meeting toward the end of the week of negotiations to prepare a list of their final demands, they ignored the Charter of Rights. Yet their demands on federal powers were substantial. A tough posture had been urged by Lévesque who had in fact circulated a draft for a common stand the night before which, with some revisions, was adopted by the premiers. Under the chairmanship of Sterling Lyon, this hard-line position became the premiers' initial collective bargaining stand, the so-called "Chateau Laurier consensus." It was, in fact, a prescription for a break down, especially surprising since the premiers knew the federal game plan as outlined in the Kirby memorandum. When the list was presented to Trudeau, many items were flatly rejected. There was little negotiation after that. By Saturday, the premiers were reading their failure speeches to the nation, assessing what had gone wrong and uniformly urging continuing discussions. Prominent among the postmortem explanations was the ill-will generated by the Kirby memorandum and the intransigence of the federal government towards the areas of provincial consensus which had painfully developed over the earlier months of negotiations. There was much talk of the collision between two competing centralized and decentralized definitions of Canada, which neither the provincial nor the federal sides were ready to compromise. But in their statements, virtually every premier but Bill Davis warned the prime minister not to resort to unilateral action, predicting that only a hollow victory could result, won at the price of defying the conventions of Canadian federalism.

With his usual astuteness, Premier Blakeney drew attention in his remarks to the conflating of the Quebec and national questions:

> I don't want to be thought to be abrasive when I say this, but as a result there were two agendas before us, one constitutional renewal for Canada and the other the continuing contest for the hearts and minds of the people of Quebec. In that latter contest, it seemed to some of us that nothing offered was enough and everything being demanded was too much.
>
> Until there is some resolution of this contest I am very much afraid that success will continue to elude us.

When Trudeau responded, it became clearer than ever that the federal government regarded the regional conception of federalism as hardly more than a variant of Quebec separatism: the idea of Canada as a "free association of provinces" was said to be shared by most of the premiers. Noting that "we hear from Premier after Premier that they agree with the concept of Canada put forward by Mr. Lévesque," Trudeau was inclined to see the national interest exclusively served by the central government and its institutions, despite Blakeney's warning that the national voice in a federation like Canada's could only be "the majority of citizens as expressed by the popular will in the House of Commons and the majority however defined of the regional will." With the charter as a tool for constraining these regional forces, Trudeau was now ready to break precedent to see his remedies for national disunity and injustice permanently entrenched in the Canadian constitution. The stage was set for unilateral action.

# 3
# Option 2: Unilateral Action

The September 1980 First Ministers' Conference had ended in failure. It was now time for the federal government to make good on its threat to go it alone. If the provinces had not believed Trudeau's pledge following the referendum victory in Quebec or his warnings afterward, they certainly could not ignore the detailed outline of a unilateral policy option contained in the leaked federal memorandum. It showed that planning for "going it alone" was well advanced, with senior cabinet ministers briefed on the full legal and political ramifications of the policy.

At the outset, the memorandum presented the cabinet with the choice of acting in federal areas of jurisdiction only or binding the provinces without their consent. If the second option were chosen, the memorandum outlined three alternative "packages" of legal intrusions and sweeteners. But the principle of intrusion into provincial areas of jurisdiction had to be faced first, after which political judgement would be required about the scale of that intrusion. If the predominantly tactical preoccupations of the memorandum were a reliable indication of federal thinking, however, debate over the principle of intrusion in a federal state was not likely to be exhaustive and sensitive. Bureaucratic advice was already structuring the policy towards binding the provinces.

Although the memorandum advised ministers that the cautious route would have the advantage of respecting convention, it presented an overwhelming number of arguments against it. Disadvantages outweighed advantages by a margin of at least five paragraphs to one. Unless the charter were binding on the provinces, rights would not be fully and universally protected. The package would be politically "meagre" especially after all the expectations built up with the negotiations and the Quebec referendum. It would "waste a once-in-a-lifetime opportunity to effect comprehensive constitutional change." It would give political advantages to Lévesque and Ryan to push on with their own unacceptable options while criticizing Ottawa, and therefore "it would be unfortunate to have to fight this criticism without in the end having a great deal to show for it." Finally, it would betray public support for the people's package. Against this weight of argument, only a daring minister would do battle with his colleagues on the issue of convention alone.

But the political forces within the cabinet and caucus might also have given a would-be cabinet rebel pause for second thoughts. The Quebec elite in the cabinet and virtually the whole Quebec contingent of 74 MPs were hawkish about putting the Parti Québécois in its place. They had won the referendum campaign and the Lévesque government was thought to be in no position to block the redressing of long-standing grievances over minority language educational rights. With the balance of power in the party so heavily based in Quebec and with virtually no representation from the West, the charter became an instrument for settling scores with the separatists and the Quebec Language Bill, and for barring similar discrimination in the other provinces. At the same time, the charter could provide a constitutional foundation for the traditional federal Liberal strategy on bilingualism and national unity. Quebec federalists enlisted the support of the English-speaking party leaders for entrenching this vision of Canada in the constitution. Such front-benchers as Allan MacEachen, Mark MacGuigan, Robert Kaplan, John Roberts and James Fleming were all reported to have demanded the entrenchment of minority language educational rights in the constitution. But having declared this a condition for Canadian constitutional renewal, they had burned their bridges with the provinces and with constitutional convention.

There was, in short, no way in which traditional Liberal politics of constitutional renewal could be carried out without violating the rights of the provinces. But once begun, the question became one of political calculation. How far must the government go to produce a politically saleable package and how far dare it intrude on provincial powers to do so? For Quebecers, "the question [was] whether . . . the protection for French outside of Quebec will fully counterbalance the protection of English within Quebec, and the degree to which the Charter will come into direct conflict with Bill 101." In other provinces, the question was one of avoiding anglophone backlash over the extension of French rights by submerging linguistic rights in a broadly based protection of *human* rights in general.

These objectives had to be balanced against the acceptable political risks with the provinces. Hence, minority language educational rights would be strongly advanced everywhere, but Trudeau himself refused to satisfy the demands of his Quebec colleagues that Ontario be declared officially bilingual. Though he had pressured Ontario privately for this concession, Trudeau knew that he needed Ontario's help and could not compel Premier Davis to give him this important prize. Compromise even on so vital a matter was essential to the success of the measure. Similarly, the cabinet worried over the scale of provincial government opposition that a fully effective Charter of Rights would provoke. They resolved that dilemma by putting in virtually all the rights of the original charter, but with all of the qualifications the provinces had suggested to weaken it. Thus, the *appearance* of an effective Charter of Rights which camouflaged linguistic and bilingual features was advanced, and a signal was relayed to the provinces that the federal government had after all taken their objections into account.

Once the federal cabinet had gone this far, there seemed little reason not to shape the amending formulae in its own favour. The preferred federal option all through the summer negotiations was the Victoria formula, but with the modification that the two Atlantic provinces must, as with the West, include at least 50 per cent of the region's population. Ottawa therefore provided that, unless an agreement was reached between governments or by a special referendum within a two-year period, the modified Victoria formula would be adopted. In addition, on amendments which affected one or more but not all provinces, it permitted change by the consent of those governments. What was far more radical however was a new provision for constitutional amendment by national referenda, an option available only to the federal government. This part of the amendment procedure allowed the federal government, in the event of deadlock with the provinces, to secure changes to the constitution whenever it garnered 51 per cent of the national vote and a specified level of support (though not necessarily a majority) in all four regions of Canada. The referendum prodecure would remain in place after two years whatever the general intergovernmental formula that might be adopted. This action stacked the cards in Ottawa's favour on all future constitutional changes.

The national Parliament was already well protected in any amendment procedure, since every formula required Ottawa's agreement. What was new in the referendum option was that Ottawa could bypass the provinces altogether, and avoid applying the same test of general intergovernmental approval to its objectives that the provinces were required to do for theirs. This referendum playing card was Ottawa's permanent substitute for unilateral recourse to Britain which, once patriation was achieved, would no longer be used. It was a feature that could dramatically centralize Canadian federalism.

By all accounts, the referendum option was pressed upon cabinet by Trudeau himself after it had been advanced by his backroom aides — Michael Kirby, Michael Pitfield and Jim Coutts. If retained as a permanent measure, it would release Ottawa from any constitutional strait-jacket in the next round of constitutional discussions and secure for all future national governments a powerful political weapon. If simply used as a negotiating device, the alternate option would warn the provinces of the dangers of obstruction or the measure itself could be used as a bargaining chip on other matters. Either way the government had crafted a device that promised grave dangers for the provinces.

As an initiative against the threats of separatism, linguistic injustice and regionalism, the package for unilateral action was a bolder attack than most had expected. Here, too, the Machiavellian virtue of decisiveness was preferred over any moderate course. The Liberals knew that they were about to enter one of the toughest political fights of the century, but they wished to keep the initiative throughout, be ready to adapt their politics and compromise as circumstances might require. Both the federal plan and its execution certainly confirmed earlier provincial suspicions about their wily adversary.

The Kirby memorandum correctly anticipated that opponents in Parliament and from the provinces "would concentrate their fire on the fact of unilateral action" and that the contents of the package would not engage the public's attention to the same extent. It also predicted a reference to the courts as a necessary complication. The government was advised to deal with both of these challenges with assurances that the resolution was proper and legal, that it was made necessary by fifty-three years of failure and that politically motivated obstruction ought not to be tolerated. It was hoped that the resolution might be pushed through Parliament and receive approval by Westminster before the courts could pronounce on it. That way the risk of an adverse judgement, which might undermine "the political legitimacy, though not the legal validity, of the patriation package," might be avoided. The government also knew that the legal position of the provinces would be much weaker after Westminster had enacted the resolution, and thought that a Canadian court would at best find the process a "violation of established conventions and therefore in one sense ... 'unconstitutional' even though legally valid."

It seems, therefore, that the government knew perfectly well that the process was questionable and possibly unconstitutional (even if technically legal) despite its numerous public statements to the contrary. Its advisers also had even correctly anticipated what the Supreme Court might have to say on the issue. But they hoped to push on brazenly in the hope that the matter could be settled politically in spite of federal-provincial conventions.

Even the management of Parliament had been carefully considered in the planning document. In a section entitled "Strategic Considerations in Parliament," the memorandum outlined a game plan for controlling the legislative process. The government was to table the resolution, permit full debate on it with a view to bringing it to a vote, and then after about two weeks of debate refer it to a joint House-Senate committee for study in apparent deference to the opposition. In this manner, the government could proceed with its budget and the "Canadianizing" National Energy Program (which promised to poison further the Parliamentary atmosphere), while the public was given an opportunity to participate in a review of the resolution. The authors of the memorandum worried about there being more "attackers" than "defenders" in committee and counselled that "careful choice of government members would be essential, and careful orchestration of hearings would be needed to ensure effective presentation of the government's position." They also felt that the matter should be safely "contained" within committee where "easier and more effective relations can be maintained with the press gallery, since relatively few reporters will follow the proceedings."

On the evening of October 2, Trudeau formally opened this phase of the constitutional struggle in a national television address outlining unilateral action. His speech was a well-crafted piece of liberal patriotism:

> It is a long and painstaking process, building a country to match a dream. But as each generation has made the sacrifices so each has reaped the rewards. Every generation of Canadians has given more than it has taken.
>
> Now it is our turn to repay our inheritance. Our duty is clear: it is to complete the foundations of our independence and of our freedoms.

With these words Trudeau fulfilled the dark prediction made by his friend, Paul Gérin-Lajoie in his classic study, *Constitutional Amendment in Canada*, published thirty years earlier. Ironically, Trudeau himself had read and commented on the manuscript and may indeed have been one of the scholars who, according to Gérin-Lajoie, had argued even then "that provincial sovereignty might be abridged .... without the consent of all provinces affected." Gérin-Lajoie thought that position was unwarranted, but openly worried whether events in Canada might not convert this scholarly view into political fact:

> Yet, this contention [federal unilateralism] might result some day — a day which may be not far distant

— in creating a trend of opinion which would make its way openly into the federal Cabinet and would finally gain the support of a majority in Parliament . . . There lies a potential source of friction between the federal Government and the provinces which is far more serious than the actual frictions of 1943 and 1944.

That day had finally come. Trudeau, the scholar-turned-politician, was about to put an academic dispute to the acid test.

In a remarkable political manoeuvre, Trudeau secured the support of one of the opposition parties even before making his public announcement, and at the same time won himself some badly needed support in the West. He talked NDP leader Ed Broadbent into committing his party, which included twenty-seven Westerners in a caucus of thirty-two. Broadbent gave his endorsement only an hour after he had seen the resolution, before he had consulted with his caucus, and in the face of a resolution to the contrary by his party's federal council. Although he held out for some changes, his praise for Trudeau's proposals — "unquestionably desirable," "sensible," "civilized" — was sweet music to Liberal ears. Although dissension within the NDP ranks followed, Trudeau had successfully isolated the Conservatives as his only implacable foe in Parliament.

Speaking on television in reply to the prime minister, Clark gave the government a sense of the debate that lay ahead:

> Because a constitution is so basic to a country, it must be the product of the broadest possible consensus. It cannot be arbitrarily imposed on this nation by only one individual or government. Nor can it be achieved through threat, ultimatum or artificial deadline. That kind of constitution-making does not serve Canada. . . .

> Mr. Trudeau tonight offers Canadians the prospect of divisive referenda, prolonged constitutional challenges in the courts, and federal-provincial turmoil. That is betrayal of those Quebeckers who voted "No" in the Quebec referendum, and all other Canadians who seek genuine renewal of our Confederation.

Since both Ontario and New Brunswick had supported a charter during the negotiations, both provinces lined up with the federal government, despite Premier Hatfield's earlier doubts about the wisdom of unilateral action and his opposition to certain features of the current resolution. Ontario's Premier Davis, noting Ottawa's concession to his province on bilingualism, equated the support of Ontario with the "sustaining of [an] effective national consensus for constitutional reform and patriation." (With eight other provinces against the federal plan, only an Ontario premier could possibly have thought that constituted "an effective national consensus.")

The grouping of political forces on the eve of the resolution battle was clear. In Parliament, the only effective opposition to unilateral action itself was that provided by the Progressive Conservatives and later by four dissident NDP MPs from Saskatchewan who broke ranks with the party on the issue. Outside Parliament, the governments in three out of four regions of the country were overwhelmingly opposed to the action: three of the Atlantic provinces, Quebec and all of Western Canada. Most of the dissident provinces began to plan concerted action including court challenges, lobbying in Britain and politicking at home. Saskatchewan's government attempted to continue talking with federal officials in the hope of improving the package, while Ottawa attempted to lure Saskatchewan away from the others with promises of including increased provincial powers over natural resources.

The debate in Parliament after October 6 went much as expected; the Conservatives fought the resolution fiercely and the NDP cemented its alliance with the Liberals in exchange for a government promise to include its earlier offer on natural resources in the package. Broadbent hoped in that way to smooth his strained relations with the NDP government in Saskatchewan and to win some credibility generally in the West; Trudeau won some badly needed support from Western MPs and divided the Parliamentary opposition. In keeping with the plan to restrict House debate to about two weeks, the government invoked closure on October 23 and sent the resolution to the Joint House-Senate Committee on the Constitution.

At this point, the federal government got a break that it had not counted on. The witnesses appearing before the committee represented almost exclusively human rights groups and governments (apart from five expert witnesses chosen by the parties) and were not nearly as critical of unilateral action as the federal memorandum had expected. The government had forgotten to take into account the popular appeal of the Charter of Rights. Although most of the public interest groups were critical of the feeble defence of rights in the resolution, they worried little about conventions or Canadian federalism. For them, the resolution did not go far enough. By catering to these demands, the government was able to strengthen its charter, to give the public the impression of flexibility and to isolate its opposition. The politics of unilateral action were made much more comfortable so long as the public fixed upon its human rights contents and not on the action itself.

This fact underlines the importance of the arena in which constitutional politics are carried out. Conducted as intergovernmental negotiations, talks on constitutional subjects like the Charter of Rights principally focus on their impact on the powers and rights of governments; conducted in a wider public forum, they are instead examined in the light of their contribution to perceived public needs. Such a conclusion seems to justify the view that governmental bargaining subverts the "people's interest," as Trudeau had so often alleged, but the matter is much more complex. The "public interest" on such a question surely must include consideration of both agendas — rights and federalism — a complex balancing act which requires an explicit role for both governmental and other public actors.

Although public participation in the constitutional process was only infrequently permitted by the governmental actors — and then only because it appeared to be politically useful, or otherwise unavoidable — the public input *was* important in shaping the eventual outcome. Hence even if the civil rights groups who appeared before the joint committee found themselves unwitting accomplices in federal political planning, their pressure was indispensable in tightening up and strengthening the Charter of Rights.

The list of groups wishing to appear before the committee was a testament to the federal strategy of grafting people's rights to federal unilateralism. The appearance of human rights' commissions, civil liberties' groups, bar associations, research institutes, and special interest groups supporting the rights of women, the handicapped, the gay community and ethnic minorities all suggested that public participation helped the federal side. Once the government saw that the committee presented no political threat, it permitted it an extension from December 9 to February 6 (later extended to February 17) and rested comfortably with the televised proceedings which had been forced by Conservative and NDP pressure. Only two of the dissenting provincial governments — Nova Scotia and Prince Edward Island — appeared before the committee, and Saskatchewan, which had not yet taken a firm position, also offered useful criticism. In neglecting this opportunity to shape public debate, the other dissenting provinces probably made Liberal management of parliamentary opinion easier.

On January 12, 1981, the committee's last witness, Justice Minister Chrétien, tabled a long list of amendments to the charter, largely at the expense of provincial arguments and interests. The amendments the government proposed, or which it later accepted from the committee or Commons, fell into four main areas: a strengthening of the Charter of Rights and Freedoms, corrections of some anomalies and unfairness in the amending formulae, recognition of native and aboriginal rights, and enlarging provincial jurisdiction, especially over natural resources. In total, these changes made for a much more saleable patriation package, even if most of the provinces and the official opposition remained against it on principle.

On the Charter of Rights, the government substituted a requirement that any limits on basic freedoms be "reasonable" rather than merely "lawful." It was therefore up to the government to justify in court limits on the citizen's right against unreasonable search or seizure, arbitrary detention or imprisonment, unjust denial of bail, and so on. New rights were written in: protection against self-incrimination, a right to be informed of the right to counsel, a right to trial by jury for major offences, and improved equality rights, especially for the mentally and physically disabled. Citizens were also given the right to seek remedies from the courts for any violations of their rights, and the courts were given the discretion to exclude evidence where it had been "obtained in a manner that infringed or denied any rights or freedoms guaranteed by this Charter."

Language guarantees were extended to new categories of citizens and better secured. Minority language educational rights were to be provided out of public funds "where numbers warrant" (in the opinion of the courts), and were extended to children of citizens who received their primary school instruction in Canada in English or French. Thus the obligations of governments to pay for minority language services was made more explicit, even if the qualification on numbers worried many advocates of bilingualism. Extending the constitutional protection of minority language education to the children of Canadian citizens who had been educated here in English or French *whatever* their original mother tongue protected the rights of many Canadians who had been overlooked in the resolution. Many other Canadians were protected in the additional provision that if one child in a family was receiving primary or secondary school instruction in English or French, all children in the family could be educated in the same language. Special arrangements were made to permit other provinces to extend language rights without going through the general amendment process. In addition to all of these changes, New Brunswick agreed to make itself a fully bilingual province under the constitution, equally entrenching the rights of citizens in both language groups.

The number of provinces required to put up an alternative amending formula to that of the federal government in a national referendum was changed from eight to seven, but the government gave this power exclusively to the legislatures (not governments) of the provinces. This "reform" was purely cosmetic, however, since the provinces still needed to meet an 80 per cent population requirement to have their alternative amending formula considered by the people; Ottawa's ally, Ontario, could block that option single-handed. A Referendum Rules Commission was established to suggest referendum guidelines for enactment by Parliament. The 50 per cent population provision for the Atlantic provinces was removed so that Prince Edward Island would not be frozen out of the process altogether (the population provision for the Western provinces was dropped in a later House amendment). A time-limit was built into the national referendum option so that Parliament was required to wait twelve months after passage of a special resolution calling for an amendment before a referendum would proceed. That provision underlined the fact that it was to be considered a "deadlock-breaking" mechanism only. Exclusive federal control over the use of referenda remained.

Native rights were specifically protected in section 25 of the charter to avoid their being set aside in order to enforce Canadians' right to equality under section 15. In a new section 33 "the aboriginal and treaty rights of the aboriginal peoples of Canada [were] recognized and affirmed." Section 33 however was capable of being amended in any province by simple agreement of that province and the federal government rather than by the general amending formula and was therefore not on as sound a footing as section

25 in the charter. To emphasize the political protection given aboriginal peoples, the government also allowed a committee amendment that within a year of proclamation the subject of aboriginal rights would be on the agenda of a constitutional conference of first ministers and that the prime minister would invite native representatives to participate in the discussion. Representatives were also required on any agenda item which the prime minister thought "directly affects" the territories. (In a gesture to Canada's policy on multiculturalism, a motherhood section 27 required the charter to be "interpreted in a manner consistent with the preservation and enhancement of the multicultural heritage of Canadians.")

The amendment giving provinces power over indirect taxation of natural resources and over interprovincial trade, with certain reservations, was advanced by NDP members on the committee and accepted by the government. It confirmed the deal offered by the federal government to the provinces in the September First Ministers' Conference. Such a provision, along with the incidental strengthening of the principle of equalization, was intended to win some badly needed support in the West and to solidify the federal NDP-Liberal alliance.

Although this change did not bring any of the Western provinces on side, a concession to the Senate eased any danger to the passage of the resolution there. The original resolution permitted the House of Commons to override the Senate whenever the Commons passed, after a ninety-day interval, a constitutional measure being held up in the second chamber. Since the Senate was threatening to block the resolution unless the offensive section was removed, Liberal members on the joint committee struck it out despite

protests by the NDP, which had a longstanding commitment to dismantle the upper house.

Meanwhile, during the joint committee hearings in
the fall of 1980 and especially during December, when
the cabinet was approving amendments to the patriation package, the federal government was attempting
to break the wall of resistance from Western Canada.
Its chosen target was Saskatchewan. Blakeney and his
affable attorney general, Roy Romanow, were well
respected by the federal leaders. Moreover, Saskatchewan had deliberately kept the channels open with
Ottawa following the threat of unilateral action in the
hope of pressing for an eventual compromise. It
seemed natural to use these channels to offer a deal to
Saskatchewan in return for its support. Negotiations
had gone well until, on February 19, Saskatchewan's
distrust of the federal government finally caused it to
pull back almost at the eleventh hour. The *Globe and
Mail* reported that Saskatchewan had deliberately
waited until the committee amendments were forthcoming to see whether the federal government would
renege on any of its understandings with Saskatchewan. When the government accepted the motion to
permit a Senate veto on constitutional amendments
and when it toyed with the Tories by accepting and
then retracting a property-rights amendment which
threatened Saskatchewan's own land control
measures, it destroyed the chances of an accord with
that province. Saskatchewan simply feared that it
would be double-crossed by the federal Liberals.

Saskatchewan was also feeling the ill will of seven
other provinces who had been caucusing over ways of
opposing Ottawa. Having begun a series of court
challenges in Manitoba, Newfoundland and Quebec,
however, they were only too happy to welcome a

somewhat chastened Saskatchewan into the legal fray. This group of provinces soon became known as the "Gang of Eight."

The essential lines of the dissident provinces' political strategy had been established in a meeting on October 14 in Toronto. The premiers were determined to resist unilateral federal action. They developed a three-pronged strategy: legal action to defeat or undermine the legitimacy of the resolution, a political campaign to turn public opinion against unilateral action, and a diplomatic offensive to scuttle the chances of passage in Britain. Over the following months of debate in Parliament and the country, these initiatives frustrated the federal attempt to get swift passage. Neither the target date of July 1, 1981, nor the carefully planned national management of the political variables was practical in the face of this opposition. Events confirmed the federal memorandum's warning that "the fight ... will be very, very rough."

The legal option was important in its own right and for its contribution to the other two parts of the strategy. Just as any citizen's intention in going to court is to "win" his or her case, the provincial governments hoped to get a ruling that the resolution was constitutionally improper, if not illegal. If it were found illegal, the federal government would be stopped. If it were found legal but improper, the political odds of forcing a compromise or fighting it successfully at home or in Britain were much more in their favour. In that sense, the provinces always had more than a purely legal purpose in mind. A court judgement carried with it the threat of political defeat or weakening of the federal position.

These political possibilities stemmed from the

provincial and federal courts' duty and power both to uphold the constitution of Canada and to answer what are called "reference" questions. The provinces reasoned that if they framed questions that tested the validity of the proposed federal resolution under the constitution of Canada, they would receive a relatively objective interpretation of the lawfulness and/or constitutional propriety of the federal action. In answering those questions, the courts would be forced to impose a ruling which would in effect either approve or reject the action.

Since the provinces could not themselves refer questions directly to the Supreme Court of Canada, the dissenting provinces decided to put their questions about the validity of the federal action to three provincial appeal courts. Their decisions could then be appealed to the Supreme Court. After agreeing on a set of reference questions asking whether, according to constitutional practice, the federal resolution required the agreement of the provinces, actions were launched over the months of October to January in appeal courts in Manitoba, Newfoundland and Quebec. Six (later eight) provinces participated in the court challenges. The three legal challenges increased the likelihood of a federal defeat or setback, and the timing of the judgements was likely to throw obstacles in the way of the July 1 objective. Finally, any delays caused by the legal questions gave the provinces time to continue the campaign for public support.

The dissenting provinces began their political opposition by threatening to stage referenda (an idea that was later dropped) and by passing resolutions in their legislatures denouncing the federal action. These resolutions gave the dissent a legislative sanction, although only in Alberta and Saskatchewan did the official opposition support the ruling party. Indeed Alberta's Progressive Conservative government found itself embarrassed when one of its members refused to support the resolution and it retaliated by expelling him from the party. To avoid supporting a Parti Québécois resolution in the Quebec National Assembly, Claude Ryan moved an amendment requiring a commitment to federalism; the PQ government rejected the amendment, which allowed Ryan to vote against the PQ motion.

The battle for public opinion was fought out both at home and in Britain. Provincial publicity campaigns were put in place (most notably in Quebec, where Ottawa countered an effective PQ campaign with a million-dollar advertising blitz in October of 1981), and many premiers spoke out on the issue as often as possible. Both Manitoba's Premier Lyon, as chairman of the Gang of Eight, and New Brunswick's Premier Hatfield, a federal ally, travelled to London to warn the British public of the grave consequences that would follow from either acceptance or rejection of the Canadian Parliament's resolution.

The lobbying effort in London began in earnest soon after the opposition strategy was put into place. Quebec took the lead with a furious campaign to warn British MPs and peers of the widespread Canadian opposition to the federal government's proposal. The federal government had already received cautious assurances from the British government concerning the resolution earlier in the summer of 1980, but it remained unclear just how the government would respond to a request from the Canadian Parliament in the face of massive provincial opposition. Britain clearly did not want to get involved in a bitter Canadian dispute nor did it want its own pressing political priorities disturbed. However federal leaders continued to state publicly that Britain would be bound to accede to any request of the Canadian Parliament to avoid "meddling" in Canadian internal affairs. Trudeau's sneering reference to British parliamentarians having "to hold their noses" while passing his measure certainly did not help improve matters in Britain. Ultimately, federal officials counted on the power of the British cabinet to get their measure through, whatever members might think of it privately.

Since the provinces could not approach the British government directly without violating diplomatic conventions, they concentrated their efforts on informing members of the British Houses of Parliament and on shaping British public opinion. They had been preceded by delegations of Canadian native peoples anxious for Britain to protect their treaty rights. In November, the political pressure moved Westminster's Select Committee on Foreign Affairs to inquire into the role which the United Kingdom ought to play on this proposed Canadian constitutional request. It received written submissions from Canadian governments and interest groups, but heard direct submissions only from British witnesses, officials and experts. British civil servants seemed to argue the federal case before the committee whereas the constitutional experts supported the provinces' contention that for the British Parliament to act as a "simple rubber-stamp" would be wrong. Ultimately, when the committee, under the chairmanship of Sir Anthony Kershaw, filed its report on January 30, 1981, it sided with the experts' view that the British Parliament ought not necessarily to act "automatically and unconditionally." Only if a request is seen to convey "the clearly expressed wishes of Canada as a federally structured whole" (either by consent of provincial governments or by regional majorities in a referendum), could the British Parliament rightfully pass any constitutional request of the Parliament of Canada.

The Kershaw report struck a hard blow at the federal government's assertion that Britain must automatically comply with any request from the Canadian Parliament. The report generated a spate of "Brit-bashing" from the federal side; Trudeau even compared it to a current science-fiction movie, *The Empire Strikes Back*. About the same time, on February 5, 1981, allegations were made in the House of Commons that the British high commissioner, Sir John Ford, had "influenced" two NDP members of Parliament by warning them that the British government was uneasy with the resolution and that it might not be given smooth passage. Leaked cables and memoranda surfaced which showed that the confident front of the federal Liberals was unwarranted. As the Parliament of Canada prepared for a renewed debate on the constitutional resolution, as amended by the joint committee, there was every indication that the fight in Britain was also going to be rough.

On February 3, however, came an important break for the Liberals and their allies which helped reverse the impact of the Kershaw report. The first of the legal decisions was announced from the Manitoba Court of Appeal. The federal side won on every one of the reference questions, although by only a three-to-two majority of the judges. That result buoyed up the federal government's supporters, despite the narrowness of the victory. It appeared to federal ministers more important than ever to push the resolution forward quickly, while the legal and political odds were still in their favour. For the Conservative opposition, the split on the Manitoba court, together with the Kershaw report, signalled the weakness of the government and the need to delay passage of the resolution until the Supreme Court of Canada's decision. In this unprecedented Parliamentary showdown the parties' political tenacity and adeptness in parliamentary procedure would be put to a severe test.

Justice Minister Chrétien moved the adoption of the resolution on February 17, 1981, promising all Canadians "a new foundation on which to build a more united, a more generous and a greater country." In reply, Jake Epp, the articulate Manitoban who was the leading Conservative representative on the joint committee, easily demonstrated the irony of this objective in the face of the "divisiveness" the resolution had already created. He asked instead that the Liberals take the constitutional route which offered the broadest consensus. Patriate the constitution with an amending formula agreeable to the provinces, he said, and leave the Charter of Rights to be added later. At the end of his speech, Epp moved an amendment to the resolution deleting the controversial national referendum option for constitutional change.

The Epp amendment occupied the House completely for more than a month. The Conservatives continued to debate it and thereby prevented either the Liberals or the NDP from putting any other amendments to the resolution. This strategy delayed proceedings and increased with every day the dangers for the Liberals of adverse shifts in public opinion and of legal attack by the courts. As the debate dragged on, the Liberals and NDP found it increasingly difficult to keep their own troops from breaking ranks. By mid-

March, one Quebec MP, Louis Duclos, and four Liberal senators had already indicated that they would not support their party's own resolution, while four NDP members from Saskatchewan (Lorne Nystrom, Simon de Jong, Doug Anguish and Stan Hovdeho) had, as early as February 19, declared that they repudiated the position to which Broadbent had committed the party. Moreover, the entire Quebec Liberal caucus was known to be exceedingly restless with the government's exemption of Ontario from bilingual status.

Challenged to submit its package to the Supreme Court for judgement, badgered for its inflexible attitude to federalism and frustrated in its attempts to proceed, the government decided to move a motion to limit debate to four more days. The motion was put by Liberal House leader Yvon Pinard on March 19. Immediately the Conservatives countered: one by one, Conservative members rose on questions of privilege or points of order to prevent any debate on Pinard's motion. For almost two weeks, the work of the House of Commons was at a standstill. The Liberals and NDP denounced the tactic and waited impatiently for the Conservatives to slip or give up.

On March 31, an appeal court in Newfoundland unlocked the parliamentary deadlock. By a unanimous vote of three, the Newfoundland court found the federal package illegal. There could be no question of proceeding until the Supreme Court had ruled on the resolution. As predicted in the federal memorandum, the Liberal government abruptly agreed to await a ruling of the Supreme Court, and promised to proceed no further with the resolution if it were found illegal by Canada's highest court. In return, the opposition was asked to cooperate in allowing the resolution to proceed through Parliament so that the court might have a finished document to examine. Final vote on the resolution itself would be withheld until the court verdict. If valid, the resolution would be put to a final vote in the House after a maximum of two days debate. The opposition agreed.

On April 23, Conservative amendments were rejected and last-minute Liberal and NDP amendments providing for sexual equality, better protections for aboriginal rights, a short preamble affirming God, and equality of the Western and Eastern provinces in the amending formula were quickly passed. Finally on April 23, 1981, the final resolution was ready, just five days before the Supreme Court was to begin hearing provincial appeals on it.

Although the federal government entered that court more cheerfully after hearing, on April 15, of the Quebec Court of Appeal's four-to-one ruling in its favour, events were certainly not unfolding as the authors of the planning documents had hoped. The political timetable was set back, the legal result was anyone's guess and, worst of all, the Parti Québécois government had decisively shed its lame-duck status. On April 13, 1981, it had won a smashing victory in the provincial elections and undermined the leadership of Liberal Claude Ryan. The result suggested that the PQ under René Lévesque had virtually as much political endurance in Quebec as the federal Liberals under Pierre Trudeau.

What the victory tended to obscure, however, was the paradox of a separatist government with no separatist mandate. As some party insiders recognized, the election results left the party in a difficult philosophical and practical position. It had to go on negotiating the federalist option with its party base committed to separatism, and it could not easily translate its political power into bargaining strength *because* of its separatist leanings. In effect, the results of the referendum lingered on. There was therefore no change in the negotiating strategy of the Quebec government, although the victory deflected its attention from the provincial Liberals and encouraged a more aggressive rhetorical assault upon Trudeau and the federal Liberals.

Only three days after his election win, bristling for a fight with Trudeau, Lévesque made a pact with the other seven dissenting premiers which he hoped would block and ultimately defeat the federal strategy. The premiers' agreement called for patriation, for an amending formula based on the Vancouver consensus and for intensive federal-provincial discussion on the other topics over a three-year period. The most important element was the adoption of the Alberta formula modified to include the possibility of transferring powers by mutual consent, financial compensation for a province opting out of amendments, and, as Table 1 shows, the placement of additional subjects in the unanimity column. Although the press treated the April 16 Constitutional Accord as a last-ditch attempt by the dissenting provinces to show that they could "agree among themselves" on a constitutional package, the deal struck that day signified much more. It demonstrated the premiers' retreat from their long-standing demands for a settlement of the division of powers prior to patriation. It tacitly signalled that bargaining on a smaller package could proceed. It signified that if bargaining were to reopen, their chief interest would be their amending formula. Since satisfaction of that demand would require from them a concession of equal importance to the federal side

(patriation having already been conceded), it invited
a trade-off with the Charter of Rights. All these developments were the results of federal unilateral
action, although the full import of the moves was not
clear even to some of the players themselves.

One government which evidently did not foresee
that it was structuring the terms of later negotiations
was Quebec. In a bold bid to foster a united bargaining position against Trudeau, Lévesque on April 16
signed away Quebec's conventional case for a veto
on future constitutional amendments. In return he
accepted the protections of an "opting out with compensation" provision along with all the other provinces. Quebec now had formally joined most other
provinces in affirming equality of the provinces in
Canada. Since this manoeuvre could not be squared
with traditional Quebec demands over amending
formulae, and since it contradicted *special status* or the
PQ's own case for Quebec's uniquely *national* status,
this move seems to have been a tactical step on which
the PQ never expected to be called to account. The
battle between Lévesque and Trudeau had by now
begun to take the form of a winner-take-all struggle
between separatism and federalism, and Lévesque
risked the long-term traditional interests of Quebec
as a constituent element in the federation for the
chance to defeat the federal unilateral action. The
odds for a separatist victory would then be much
stronger. But such brinkmanship was all the more
daring since it was not needed to preserve the opposition to the federal Liberals and since the federal government had already said earlier that, while it found
the Vancouver amending formula "obnoxious," it
could live with it. It seemed Lévesque and his minister
of intergovernmental affairs, Claude Morin, who as

civil servant or politician had taken part in all the constitutional meetings of the previous twenty years, did not consider the prospects of federal compliance with their amending formula. They therefore did not see the necessary quid pro quo — the entrenchment of the Charter of Rights.

But until the verdict was in on unilateral action, it was unlikely there would be any bargaining. Each side struggled for outright victory. It was not until after a Supreme Court ruling some five months later that talk of negotiations based on the April 16 accord was again heard.

# 4
# The Supreme Court Decision

When the Supreme Court assembled on September 28, 1981, to render judgement on the federal patriation package, all participants knew that a milestone in the struggle over the constitution was about to be passed. After almost a year of bitter debate throughout the country, many of the issues were going to be settled. Did the package diminish provincial powers? Was it constitutionally proper to proceed without provincial consent? Were all or indeed any parts of the package legal? Disagreements among experts and the often strident arguments of political elites at the national and regional levels on *both* sides of these questions had left the country unsure about the acceptability and lawfulness of Parliament's resolution. What heightened the uncertainty were the split decisions coming from appeal courts in Manitoba, Newfoundland and Quebec, which had given the federal government a lead of merely two to one. Moreover, of the thirteen appeal court judges who heard the case, *seven* had sided with the federal government and *six* with the arguments of the provinces. There was no reason to think that the Supreme Court decision might not also be a cliffhanger.

The political stakes in this decision were higher than they had been in any constitutional question put before the courts since Confederation. But its gravity and political significance were easy to overlook. With all of the political propaganda and simplistic talk over a Charter of Rights, it was easy to miss the profound nature of the federal package, both for what it said about the constitutional process in Canada and, equally important, for what it contained in political substance.

The question of *process* was raised by unilateral action itself. It pointed to a breakdown in the rules of the game, to the failure of governments to work within the tacit understandings of Canadian federalism to resolve political differences. Although such a departure from the ground rules might be justified by any number of arguments, unilateralism itself suggested that the mutual trust and respect needed to make federalism work in Canada were rapidly disappearing. At the end of the negotiating sessions with the provinces in September 1980, the federal government had already shown a lack of confidence in federalism by labelling so many other governments as separatist or crypto-separatist. Unilateral action was then a foregone conclusion, since according to this view Canada could only be preserved through the national government. Acting on that presumption, Ottawa deliberately polarized public opinion with its charge that federalism did not work and challenged the provinces to stop it. The provinces responded to the challenge in part by referring this assault upon federalism to the courts.

Many thought it unwise to refer so highly "political" a matter to judges. But they forgot that Canada and other federal countries had been dropping political hot potatoes onto the courts for a long time. When power is divided by the constitution between two levels of government, the courts always act as umpires, often in delicate political circumstances. For example, the Supreme Court had not long before (in 1976) heard a dispute over federal wage and price controls. If the Supreme Court rules against a government's law, the lower courts simply refuse to enforce it. In general, of course, the court assumes that if any government breaks the constitutional rules it does so accidentally.

In this case, however, the political intent to change the powers of governments especially with the entrenched charter could hardly be ignored. The issue then confronted the court squarely: How was it to discharge its umpiring role? How was it to treat a federal action so apparently inconsistent with the theory and practice of federalism? The matter of *process* raised issues of the highest order in judicial review and invited the court for the first time to define its methods, values and styles of decision making in uncharted legal areas.

On the question of *substance*, the so-called people's package contained political dynamite. It overruled some parts of the Quebec language bill, the cornerstone of the PQ government, and sought to abolish permanently a century of discrimination against minority language educational rights elsewhere in Canada. It also aimed to extend and to entrench bilingualism, to eliminate provincial obstacles to a national labour market, to establish a Charter of Rights which would grant courts the power to "legislate" on moral and social issues, to expose many past and future statutes on provincial and federal books to possible legal challenge, and to impose terms for amending formulae which included, in the event of deadlock, exclusive federal use of referenda to carry out constitutional change over the heads of provincial governments. These were constitutional measures with far-reaching and unpredictable effects. But if American practice was any guide, the charter and other provisions of the resolution would tilt power decisively toward the national capital and begin to reverse the decentralized character of Canadian federalism.

For the Supreme Court, it was an uncomfortable challenge. The questions before it permitted in law either a narrow, technical response, which would evade the broader issues, or a much more expansive answer. If the court chose to address the underlying issues, its answers would define the principles of Canada as a federal state, the status of the unwritten rules which govern the exercise of legal power and, more broadly, the role of the court itself as a guardian of the federal pact. Thus, the reputation of the court itself was at stake at a time when it was a constitutional subject of federal-provincial bargaining. Ironically, the judges were also expected to rule on the validity of a federal action of which *they* were the chief beneficiaries. If, as all the critics were saying, the federal resolution would give the courts much more power, was it not odd that the judiciary would have a decisive say in approving or rejecting it?

## Issues and Legal Strategies

The Supreme Court was asked to rule specifically on
reference questions put before appeal courts by the
provinces of Manitoba, Newfoundland and Quebec
— questions designed to test the constitutionality of
the proposed federal resolution. Reference cases permit the government using them to draft questions
which draw out issues of fact, law and convention on
which it desires a ruling. To initiate a reference then
gives a government a powerful strategic advantage: it
reserves to itself the power to define the issues which
the court is expected to answer. That government
whose actions are the object of the reference is by the
same token placed at a disadvantage, since it must
fight its case on terms set by a legal adversary.

Although the questions from each of the provinces
were not exactly the same, they were all designed to
test three things. Did the federal constitutional resolution affect provincial rights, powers and privileges?
Was there a constitutional convention requiring provincial consent for constitutional resolutions affecting
provincial powers, rights and privileges? Is the agreement of the provinces "constitutionally required" for
such amendments? The reference case was not directed
toward settling the question of the *legality* of the
federal proposal (the question that would have suited
federal interests best), but its *constitutional propriety*
or *legitimacy* (the question that suited the provinces
best).

From the point of view of the public interest, it is
just as well that the broad set of questions was referred
to the court. A decision on the narrower ground of
legality would not have answered the moral and

political concerns about how amendments affecting federal-provincial powers ought to be conducted. That larger matter had by now become a part of the national debate. Canadians were not interested merely in legal mechanisms but in the principles and practices surrounding this kind of change.

Just as the terms of the court battle were set by the provincial reference questions, they also shaped the legal strategies developed by the federal and provincial governments. Ottawa was determined to downplay the significance of the first two questions in the reference and to treat the third as though it were simply a legal question. As it declared in its Supreme Court factum (its written statement on the issues and legal arguments), the essential issue was whether Parliament's resolution had "the force of law in Canada." It argued that since that was the fundamental matter, answers to questions one and two would become unnecessary and irrelevant. In this manner, federal attorneys hoped to influence the judges' disposition of the questions in a way that would be closer to what Ottawa would have put to the court had it initiated the reference. Such a strategy assumed that a forceful argument, which focused the question in the desired direction, would shape the hearing in court and the eventual judgement.

Of course, this plan did not permit the federal government to ignore the first two questions but merely to belittle their significance. This strategy was pursued with great skill and erudition, but counsel was unable to persuade enough appeal court judges to rule decisively in Ottawa's favour. By the time of the Supreme Court hearing, federal attorneys were attributing errors in lower court judgements to judicial confusions over law and convention. There was throughout the federal factum a distinctly confident and instructive tone.

Although the dissenting provinces had caucused over the questions put to the appeal courts, the quality of their factums varied sharply as each of the attorneys general handed the legal assignment to their deputies and staff and/or to local legal notables. No attempt was made to establish a joint research bureau staffed by leading constitutional lawyers and scholars who might match the experience and stature of noted Toronto lawyer J.J. Robinette, one of those advising the federal government. With as many as eight provincial governments participating, the possibilities of a uniform legal strategy were slim. But the disunity made it possible for distinctive approaches to be taken by some provinces, notably Saskatchewan.

In general, the provinces spent their time establishing the effects of the resolution on provincial powers, the existence of conventions and the general implications of the proposed federal action for a federal state like Canada. Although this strategy exposed them many times to criticism about the *political* nature of their submission, it had the virtue of reminding the courts of their special umpiring responsibility in a federal state and of the need to take a larger view of the matter. By underlining the importance of the second question in particular, the provinces could challenge the constitutional legitimacy of unilateral action.

### Arguments and Judgement: Question One

*If the amendments to the Constitution of Canada sought in the "Proposed Resolution for a Joint Address to Her Majesty the Queen respecting the Constitution of Canada," or any of them, were enacted, would federal-*

*provincial relationships or the powers, rights or privileges granted or secured by the Constitution of Canada to the provinces, their legislatures or governments be affected and if so, in what respect or respects?*

In all the appeal court hearings, federal counsel had insisted, as it did in its factum to the Supreme Court of Canada, that the court ought not to answer this question on the grounds that it was "speculative" and "premature." When, for example, the Manitoba and Newfoundland courts were questioning the matter, the resolution was being amended and revised as a result of parliamentary study. It was premature then to ask a court to pass on whether it affected provincial powers and, if so, in what respects. Manitoba's appeal court by a majority of three to two accepted the federal argument but the appeal court of Newfoundland by a unanimous vote did not. The Newfoundland court thought there was sufficient substance in the resolution as it then stood to answer the first question. Once the resolution was finalized in Parliament and after Quebec's appeal court also rejected the federal contention, the federal position became harder to maintain. Yet even in its factum to the Supreme Court, the attorney general of Canada insisted that the question was "too vague" and "too general" and thus it was "impossible to give a general answer."

The factum went on to assert rather extraneous political points that had come up earlier in debates in Parliament: that the resolution increased the powers of the provinces by giving them a lawful status in future constitutional amendments; that it "will submit the exercise of certain of their legislative powers to objective standards" (presumably a supercilious reference to court reviews of provincial laws as they relate to human rights); and that no "transfer of legislative competence to the prejudice of the provinces" was involved. This political blustering was to no avail in the Supreme Court hearing, where the federal government finally conceded that the answer to question one had to be yes. In its ruling on September 28, after excusing the Manitoba court for refusing to answer the question earlier, the Supreme Court voted yes unanimously, without expounding on which provincial powers were affected.

## Arguments and Judgement: Question Two

*Is it a constitutional convention that the House of Commons and Senate of Canada will not request Her Majesty the Queen to lay before the Parliament of the United Kingdom of Great Britain and Northern Ireland a measure to amend the Constitution of Canada affecting federal-provincial relationships or the powers, rights or privileges granted or secured by the Constitution of Canada to the Provinces, their legislatures or governments without first obtaining the agreement of the provinces?*

The answer to the first question was much simpler than the answers to either of the other two. Since the third question asked the court to rule on whether provincial consent was "constitutionally required" for amendments affecting provincial powers or federal-provincial relations, the answer to the second question on the existence of a constitutional convention was crucial for judgement on the third.

For that reason, the federal government's legal strategy, which first sought to bracket the second question as "inappropriate for judicial determination," was a shrewd one. But, because of their irrelevant nature, none of the arguments advanced to shut out court consideration of the second question were successful with *any* members of the Supreme Court. The first argument was that the court ought not to answer because the resolution concerned a matter of "internal parliamentary procedure" over which courts exercised no jurisdiction. In a sweeping claim of immunity reminiscent of arguments advanced for "executive privilege" in the United States, Ottawa's attorneys attempted to shield from court review Parliament's right to pass resolutions on *anything* it liked. Not a single judge accepted this argument since it in effect denied any role for conventions under the smoke-screen of Parliament's internal rights and privileges. The second argument was that because the question concerned matters of "political exigency and not law or convention" the court ought not to answer it. Although the political nature of conventions as defined in reference question two was acknowledged by the Supreme Court, this did not lead *any* of the justices to discard the question on that ground alone. The third and fourth arguments were essentially that, since conventions were themselves hard to define clearly and since they were also imprecise and flexible, they were entirely unsuitable objects for courts. Those arguments, too, did not pose any barrier to the court answering the question.

The second stage of the federal legal strategy was to deny the existence of the alleged convention. In the provincial appeal courts, this part of their strategy had been upheld (with some dissents) in two of the three courts; only Newfoundland's court rejected outright the federal arguments. The lawyers for the attorney general of Canada prepared this part of their case with a massive and well-conceived review of *all* previous Canadian constitutional amendments in any way affecting provincial rights and powers either directly or indirectly. The review showed that no uniform practice of consulting the provinces had ever developed and that therefore no convention or rule to that effect existed. This mode of organizing the material and drawing from it the desired conclusion suited federal purposes perfectly, even though there were important distinctions that could be drawn between different kinds of amendments. For example, an amendment which in 1930 finally granted to the Western provinces control over their lands and natural resources (which other provinces had always enjoyed) was by its nature non-contentious so far as the other provinces were concerned; it did not directly affect all provinces' legislative powers in the same way that ceding jurisdiction over unemployment insurance or old age pensions to the federal level did. By treating all amendments alike and by noting the various procedures that were adopted for amendment in each instance, the federal government appeared to overturn any sense that a working convention requiring provincial consent existed.

The statements of responsible actors such as former federal ministers were frequently used by federal attorneys to show that although it was undoubtedly politically desirable to secure provincial consent to constitutional amendments affecting the provinces, there was no requirement to do so. This position was buttressed by the argument "that in no case has the United Kingdom Parliament refused to enact an amendment to the B.N.A. Act on the ground that provincial consents have not been given." (The argument conveniently ignored the fact that no previous resolution had ever gone forward with massive provincial opposition.) The "non-existence of the alleged convention" was also demonstrated by the fact that it could not be defined: federal counsel claimed that it could not be determined whom such a convention would bind, when it had come into existence, what kinds of amendments it covered, or what degree of provincial consent was required. In the absence of any certainty and precision on these points, the attorney general of Canada argued that no convention of the type raised in question two existed.

Finally, the third stage of the federal strategy was to argue that even if a convention existed, it was not legally enforceable. Thus a convention might be recognized especially as an aid to the interpretation of a legal issue (in the same sense that "courts 'recognize' that people usually sleep at night and are awake during the day"), but it could not lead to court "declaration" of such a convention; such a task was fit "for politicians and political scientists, not the courts." A vast number of constitutional authorities and precedents were marshalled to show that no respectable constitutional authority (with the exception of W.R. Lederman, former dean of law at Queen's University), would support the idea that conventions were rules which courts could legally impose upon anyone.

All the provinces recognized that success on question two was essential to winning at least a moral and political victory and possibly a legal victory on the third question as well. In the appeal courts, the provinces too had busied themselves with scores of statements by cabinet ministers, prime ministers and British parliamentarians showing that there was a rule requiring provincial consent to constitutional amendments affecting provincial powers. They brought together all the constitutional amendments which showed that this was a consistent practice, especially since the Statute of Westminster was passed in 1931.

They did not however develop an effective response to the federal government's apparently overwhelming case that the practice of consultation was variable, extending from unanimous consent on some amendments to no consent on others. For that reason, the provincial case did not fare well on question two in either Manitoba or Quebec. Even with those justices who dissented, there was evidence of discomfort with the counting-up-amendments approach; they chiefly relied on the contention that after 1931 the provinces enjoyed a legal status as equal and sovereign partners with Ottawa in a federal system of government.

The more forceful of the provincial factums attempted to draw out the absurdity of Ottawa's contentions by showing that the central government was claiming an absolute legal power to do whatever it might wish to the constitution of Canada. If Ottawa's arguments were correct, it could unilaterally convert the country from a federal to a unitary state, strike down the use of the French language in Quebec or transfer the control over natural resources to itself. Such power at the centre could not be squared with the principles of a federal state.

By the time of the Supreme Court hearing, Saskatchewan had joined the other provinces in the legal battle and presented through its attorney, Ken Lysyk, a much more defensible legal argument on question two than the courts had yet seen. Saskatchewan's counsel saw with much more clarity the use the federal government was making of the practice on all the constitutional amendments and at the outset of its submission proceeded to cut the Gordian knot.

> It is submitted that the questions before the Court in this Reference in essence, although not in terms,

address a specific class of constitutional amendment, namely, those amendments which change provincial legislative powers under the Canadian constitution. Accordingly, it will be further submitted, the central issue is *whether there is a constitutional convention or constitutional requirement for agreement of the provinces to amendments which change provincial legislative powers.* It is therefore unnecessary to address the broader, and very different question of amendments to the British North American acts, 1867-1975 generally. Indeed, to approach the matter in terms of examining all amendments to the B.N.A. act, as an undifferentiated group, tends to obscure the central issue raised in this Reference.

Saskatchewan then proceeded to sever those amendments that touched federal-provincial relations only indirectly from those that did so directly. Only the latter class of amendment was pertinent. This was an astute counter-attack on the federal government's principal case against the existence of the convention. There was no question that the provinces were chiefly contesting amendments which directly affected their powers and that the federal explanation of the practice on other kinds of amendments was quite deliberately obscuring that issue. Once Saskatchewan had established that point, it went on to show that there was with respect to this class of amendment a clear convention: the precedents allowed for no exceptions, the actors in the precedents treated the convention as binding and the convention itself rested upon a sound rationale. Thus, the usual tests for establishing the existence of a convention were met.

The contribution of the Saskatchewan factum did not end there however. After showing that every amendment since Confederation which touched directly on provincial legislative powers proceeded only with the consent of the affected province or provinces, Saskatchewan pointed out the errors of justices Samuel Freedman and Roy Matas of the Court of Appeal of Manitoba on three points: their failure to distinguish between classes of amendments, their consequent failure to see that uniform practice as well as a 1965 federal government white paper on the subject had sanctioned the convention of provincial consent, and their failure to interpret correctly the section of the federal white paper sanctioning the rule. It was the last oversight which was of tremendous importance not only to the existence of the convention, but also to the unanimity rule to which all dissenting provinces but Saskatchewan were committed.

Justice Freedman had argued that the federal white paper in 1965 entitled *The Amendment of the Constitution of Canada* did not disclose and confirm a convention in the following three-sentence section:

> *The fourth general principle is that the Canadian Parliament will not request an amendment directly affecting federal-provincial relationships without prior consultation and agreement with the provinces.* This principle did not emerge as early as others but since 1907, and particularly since 1930, has gained increasing recognition and acceptance. *The nature and the degree of provincial participation in the amending process, however, have not lent themselves to easy definition.*

In particular, Justice Freedman argued that the third sentence contradicted and negated the first. Saskatchewan countered in the following way:

> It is respectfully submitted that Chief Justice Freedman erred in this analysis. The third sentence

is concerned not with the *existence* of a principle (or convention) but with the *measure of provincial agreement* ("the nature and the degree of provincial participation") that is necessary with respect to this kind of constitutional amendment. The distinction is of considerable importance and it relates to [Saskatchewan's] position that...there is both a constitutional convention and a constitutional requirement that the agreement of the provinces be obtained for a proposed constitutional amendment changing legislative powers, but that it does not follow that the agreement of *all* the provinces must be obtained.

Supporting this conclusion with quotation from Prime Minister William Lyon Mackenzie King on a 1940 amendment, Saskatchewan concluded that there may be "some uncertainty on whether unanimity is necessary, but none on whether substantial provincial support is necessary." This legal argument seriously eroded the federal case.

When the court's answer to question two was revealed on September 28, 1981, a clear split emerged between the judges with six voting yes and three voting no. Justices Ronald Martland, Roland Ritchie, Brian Dickson, Jean Beetz, Julien Chouinard and Antonio Lamer united to give the provinces a "win" by declaring that there *was* a convention or rule which required substantial provincial consent for Ottawa's constitutional resolution. Therefore unilateral action by the federal Parliament would be "unconstitutional in the conventional sense." Chief Justice Bora Laskin and justices Willard Estey and William McIntyre ruled that no such convention existed and therefore that the national government could proceed without any legal *or* constitutional concern for provincial consent. Thus, the decision of the Newfoundland Court of Appeal on the second question was upheld and that of the appeal courts of Manitoba and Quebec rejected. Doubts remained, however. How was the split to be explained? How could the members of the court disagree so sharply on a matter of this importance?

Before the reasons for judgement are assessed, one should recall that divisions within the court are not unusual. Since matters come before the court mostly because they are questions over which reasonable men might differ, they are by their nature non-technical. They call on the judges' reason, experience and philosophy. In addition, judges are human; they necessarily bring their political biases and personal values to their work, even though they are expected to exercise unusual self-restraint in this respect. Therefore two (and sometimes more) quite defensible answers may be given to any question before the court and the values or principles on which such answers are based clearly laid out.

Although it was evident that the majority and the dissenters were at loggerheads over many matters of law and principle, the issues over which they fought were essentially defined by the factums of Saskatchewan and the federal government. Just as these two adversaries, personified in co-chairmen Chrétien and Romanow's friendly "Tuque and Uke" show, tended to dominate the political negotiations of the 1980 summer, the same antagonists took the limelight in court. The majority of the Supreme Court inclined to favour Saskatchewan, while the dissenters, after brushing aside the first part of the federal legal strategy, followed pretty faithfully the federal line of argument concerning the non-existence of conventions.

Saskatchewan had provided the first bone of contention between two factions of the court by refusing to treat the second question as though it were a test of the unanimity rule. Saskatchewan argued that the question merely enquired into the existence of a convention requiring provincial consent for those matters described in the question, without reference to the exact measure of consent required; the federal government had treated the second question as though it were asserting a convention requiring unanimous consent. The issue was an important one. If a convention requiring unanimity was being advanced, it would be easier to show that there was no consistent practice or agreement and therefore no such convention. If the reference question was not asserting unanimity, the case for such a convention was much stronger.

The dissenting judges thought that the reference question clearly asked for a convention requiring the agreement of all the provinces, as every party but Saskatchewan was alleging, and that it was that question and that question only which must be answered. In their reasons, the dissenters bluntly pointed a finger at the majority of their brethren for "editing the questions to develop a meaning not clearly expressed." Declaring that the words "of the provinces" in the reference question "in this context and in general usage mean in plain English all of the Provinces of Canada," it concluded that "the Court may answer only the questions put and may not conjure up questions of its own which, in turn, would lead to uninvited answers."

The majority bloc replied to that scolding by declaring that the question did not and could not be read as though the last part of the question had read "of all the provinces."

It would have been easy to insert the word "all" into the question had it been intended to narrow its meaning. But we do not think it was so intended. The issue raised by the question is essentially whether there is a constitutional convention that the House of Commons and Senate of Canada will not proceed alone.

After pointing out as well that the Quebec reference question clearly pointed to "something less than unanimity," the majority suggested that if there were ambiguity in the question, the court "should not in a constitutional reference be in a worse position than that of a witness in a trial and feel compelled simply to answer Yes or No." There were clear precedents in earlier reference cases to show that the court should not be a victim of any misleading wording or possible misunderstandings.

Striking differences also arose between the two factions over the role and significance of convention in a federal state. Although both sides agreed with Justice Freedman of Manitoba that

- a convention occupies a position somewhere in between a usage or custom on the one hand and a constitutional law on the other,
- [that it is] nearer to law than to usage or custom,
- [that it] "is a rule which is regarded as obligatory by the officials to whom it applies" and
- that the sanction for breach of a convention will be political rather than legal,

they still did not agree to give to conventions the same *constitutional status* in a federal state. This dispute went to the root of their philosophical differences over the Canadian state.

The majority bloc began by describing conventions

as those largely unwritten rules which, for example, compel the government's resignation when the opposition gains a majority at the polls or dictate the queen's or governor general's exercise of legal power only on advice of ministers. Such conventional rules are not enforceable by the courts, since they do not form part of the law of the constitution. But noncompliance with the first convention could "be regarded as tantamount to a coup d'état," while noncompliance with the second would produce a "political crisis." Conventions therefore "ensure that the legal framework of the Constitution will be operated in accordance with the prevailing constitutional values or principles." Thus they "may be more important than some laws. Their importance depends on that of the value or principle which they are meant to safeguard."

Since the majority had agreed with the dissenters that such conventions could not be enforced by the courts, it appeared that conventions could none the less be discarded whenever politicians felt strong enough to do so. To provide a constitutional sanction against such action, the majority proceeded to label any violation of such conventions "unconstitutional." Such a declaration could not make any legal difference, but its moral and political force would be considerable. In this way, the majority of the court went as far as they could in giving conventions in a federal state the maximum defence possible. This part of the majority decision was daring and well-conceived:

> [Conventions] form an integral part of the Constitution and of the constitutional system. They come within the meaning of the word "Constitution" in the preamble of the British North America Act, 1867:

> Whereas the Provinces of Canada, Nova Scotia, and New Brunswick have expressed their Desire to be federally united...with a Constitution similar in principle to that of the United Kingdom;

That is why it is perfectly appropriate to say that to violate a convention is to do something which is unconstitutional although it entails no direct legal consequence. But the words "constitutional" and "unconstitutional" may also be used in a strict legal sense, for instance with respect to a statute which is found *ultra vires* or unconstitutional. The foregoing may perhaps be summarized in an equation: constitutional conventions plus constitutional law equal the total Constitution of the country.

The dissenters were moved by a different spirit. After reiterating what the majority had conceded about the non-legal status of convention, the dissenters went on to remove any constitutional status for conventions. They declared that the "observance" of a convention could not be made a constitutional requirement even in the non-legal sense. "In a federal state where the essential feature of the Constitution must be the distribution of powers between the two levels of government, each supreme in its own legislative sphere, *constitutionality and legality must be synonymous, and conventional rules will be accorded less significance than they may have in a unitary state such as the United Kingdom.*" This conclusion suggested that, even if the dissenters had agreed that a convention requiring provincial support existed, they would have been unwilling to give it constitutional significance. Why legality should exclude a role for conventions in a federal as opposed to unitary state was also not really explained. The dissenters' argument was, on the face of it, a blanket exclusion of a court's role in recognizing the constitutional functions of conventions. This left conventions (even those with legitimate constitutional features) as purely political matters, as the federal government had been contending. If the dissenters were required to put their views "in an equation," it would have amounted to: the *law* is the *constitution*.

Thus the two blocs on the court centred on the views of the Canadian state of the Saskatchewan and federal governments respectively: the importance of constitutional convention and the federal principle versus the strict question of law and an "imperfect" more centralized federalism. Such a division of philosophy was clear over the demands of a convention itself: the majority was able to separate the *principle* of provincial consent from the *measure* of consent required and insisted that to demand that a convention have the precision of a legal rule was "tantamount to denying that this area of the Canadian Constitution is capable of being governed by conventional rules." The minority group argued that lack of precision over "fixing the degree of provincial participation . . . robs any supposed convention of that degree of definition which is necessary to allow for its operation." The majority simply replied that if "a consensus had emerged on the measure of provincial agreement, an amending formula would quickly have been enacted and we would no longer be in the realm of conventions."

When the majority offered its reason for the convention, it came quickly to the heart of the matter: unilateral action was inconsistent with the *federal* nature of Canada.

> The federal principle cannot be reconciled with a state of affairs where the modification of provincial legis-

lative powers could be obtained by the unilateral action of the federal authorities. It would indeed offend the federal principle that "a radical change to [the] constitution [be] taken at the request of a bare majority of the members of the Canadian House of Commons and Senate."

The purpose of this conventional rule is to protect the federal character of the Canadian Constitution and prevent the anomaly that the House of Commons and Senate could obtain by simple resolution what they could not validly accomplish by statute.

The dissenting judges rejected this argument on four grounds:

• that a convention providing for partial provincial consent would not protect federalism since "those provinces favouring amendment would be pleased while those refusing consent could claim coercion";

• that unanimous consent, while protecting federalism in theory, would "overlook...the [centralized] nature of Canadian federalism which is neither 'perfect' nor 'ideal,'" i.e., Ottawa enjoys legal power to strike down provincial laws ("disallowance") or to seize provincial property ("declaratory power"), etc.

• that unilateral action would protect the "federal state without disturbing the distribution or balance of power and enshrine provincial rights" in a new amending formula;

• that the threat to Canadian federalism (i.e., to convert Canada into a unitary state) was purely hypothetical and not actually before the court and that in any case "it is not for the Court to express views on the wisdom or lack of wisdom of these proposals."

Since the convention required "substantial provincial support," it would seem that the dissenters' first argument that federalism would not be protected was a trifle far-fetched. It confused a province's sense of coercion with the degree of provincial participation needed to pass the "federal" test. All the others were essentially arguments advanced by the federal government, and the majority of the court had this to say about them:

> It is true that Canada would remain a federation if the proposed amendments became law. But it would be a different federation made different at the instance of a majority in the Houses of the federal Parliament acting alone. It is this process itself which offends the federal principle.

From that position, the majority of six answered yes to the second question and declared further that "the agreement of the provinces of Canada, no views being expressed as to its quantification, is *constitutionally required* for the passing of the... resolution... and that the passing of this resolution without such agreement would be *unconstitutional in the conventional sense*." (Emphasis added.)

### Arguments and Judgement: Question Three

*Is the agreement of the provinces of Canada constitutionally required for amendment to the Constitution of Canada where such amendment affects federal-provincial relationships or alters the powers, rights or privileges granted or secured by the Constitution of Canada to the provinces, their legislatures or governments?*

It would appear that the last words of the majority on question two also answered question three: yes, the agreement of the provinces was required. This decision however was qualified by the words, "in the conventional sense," and the third question was thought to ask if the agreement of the provinces was also required *by law*. Thus to deal with the distinct elements of law and convention, the court felt that it had to split the question into two parts. The requirement of provincial agreement by constitutional convention was then brought forward from question two to answer the first part of question three.

To answer the *legal* requirement of provincial consent, the court reformed into a new alignment of seven judges who said no and two judges who said yes. Among the no faction of the court were the three dissenters (Laskin, Estey and McIntyre) who had rejected the second question. They were joined by four of the justices who had formed the majority on question two, justices Dickson, Beetz, Chouinard and Lamer. This new majority declared that strictly speaking the law did not require provincial consent. On this issue alone, the federal attorneys had scored a "win."

How was it possible that this "swing" group of four justices could answer question three in a split way: yes, provincial consent is required by convention; no, it is not required by law? It was clear from that group's position on question two that winning on the matter of convention would not mean winning on law, because the courts could not enforce conventions as though they were legal rules. If a convention were improperly violated by those with legal authority, the courts would still "be bound to enforce the law, not the convention." The remedy for violation of convention would have to be a political sanction.

The provinces, especially Manitoba, had attempted to argue that the conventional rule in question two had "crystallized" into a rule of law. Quoting from an extensive series of cases and authorities, they sought to limit Parliament's legal power to draft such a resolution and to limit the Parliament of the United Kingdom from complying with such a resolution if it did not carry provincial consent. The majority rejected these arguments. They declared that to argue otherwise would distort the case law and established opinion and invite the court into the odd position that Canada had always had an amending formula:

> It would be anomalous indeed, overshadowing the anomaly of a Constitution which contains no provision for its amendment, for this Court to say retroactively that in law we have had an amending formula all along, even if we have not hitherto known it; or, to say that we have had in law one amending formula, say from 1867 to 1931, and a second amending formula that has emerged after 1931.

Drawing on the Statute of Westminster and on statements in conferences prior to it, the provinces had argued that Britain had given up legal authority to amend the Canadian constitution in the way in which Ottawa was contending, and that it could do so now only on the advice of the "proper constitutional authorities." If the amendment touched provincial powers or interests, those authorities would be the provincial legislatures or governments. The majority dismissed this argument: "it distorts both history and ordinary principles of statutory or constitutional interpretation." The parliaments of Canada and the United Kingdom retained unlimited legal power to proceed without provincial consent.

Manitoba had advanced an interesting argument that Ottawa "cannot do indirectly what it cannot do directly." Since it could not pass the resolution on its own, "it would be illegal to invoke United Kingdom authority to do for Canada what it cannot do itself."

Although the court majority rejected this argument on the grounds that it "confused the issue of process . . . with the legal competence of the British Parliament," the Manitoba submission drew attention to the colourable or specious nature of the federal position. Similar arguments had frequently formed the basis of Privy Council decisions and they deserved a more thoughtful response than they received from the majority.

The final general contention of the provinces had been that the Parliament of Great Britain must take account of the federal nature of Canada. The provinces were equal and sovereign in their own sphere of legislative authority, and therefore any federal unilateral action which limits provincial powers must be found illegal. The court must "project externally, as a matter of law, the internal distribution of legislative power." The majority refused to do so even though the two dissenters on the court, justices Martland and Ritchie, reminded them that Parliament's treaty-making powers had been limited in precisely that manner by the Privy Council in the 1937 Labour Conventions case. In that decision, the court had ruled that Ottawa could not escape the division of legislative powers merely by signing an international agreement promising to enact certain labour measures which ordinarily fell under provincial jurisdiction; the federal principle limited Ottawa's ability to do what it liked in its external commitments. But the Supreme Court decided that the law, as distinct from convention, provided no shelter for federalism. "The law knows nothing of any requirement of provincial consent, either to a resolution of the federal Houses or as a condition of the exercise of United Kingdom legislative power."

Such a conclusion was more than justices Martland and Ritchie could accept. They insisted that Ottawa's assertion of absolute legal power "to cause the B.N.A. Act to be amended in any way they desire" was inconsistent with the federal character of Canada's constitution. The preservation of the federal nature of the country was a "dominant principle of Canadian constitutional law" which it was the primary duty of the court to address and defend.

> In our opinion, the two Houses lack legal authority, of their own motion, to obtain constitutional amendments which would strike at the very basis of the Canadian Federal system, i.e. the complete division of legislative powers between the Parliament of Canada and the Provincial Legislatures. It is the duty of this Court to consider this assertion of rights with a view to the preservation of the Constitution.

The dissenters showed that the courts had developed principles to defend federalism in unprecedented circumstances even where there were no express provisions for such principles in the BNA Act. In each case, these principles flowed from the federal nature of Canada's constitution and were given "full legal force in the sense of being employed to strike down legislative enactments." There was therefore no excuse for taking a timid position on the legal question any more than on the matter of convention. Whatever statutory authority Parliament had to pass resolutions requesting amendments to the constitution, it "excluded the power to do anything inconsistent with the B.N.A. Act." Although the dissenters also accepted other technical arguments for upholding the provinces, it was essentially the federal principle which they thought required legal recognition and protection.

The Martland-Ritchie dissent, founded on a broader set of concerns arising out of Canadian constitutional law, did not draw a thoughtful response from the court majority. The majority view, its attention distracted by the sharp distinctions between convention and law, did not appear to consider seriously what legal impediments federalism placed upon the doctrine of the unlimited sovereignty of Parliament. In effect, having severed law from convention, they concluded that there was no obstacle to Parliament legally proceeding with a constitutionally improper measure. This is an unusual posture for any court to have adopted in a federal state. The clear implication is that the principle of federalism itself has no legal force even where a government action, to use the majority language on question two, "offends the federal principle." It is difficult to make that conclusion square with the fact that the Privy Council, the British court that served as Canada's final court of appeal on constitutional cases until 1949, had given the federal principle legal force in several landmark decisions. These cases and rationale were produced by Martland and Ritchie, but the best that the majority could do in reply was to say that federalism would remain intact in spite of this measure, and that Canada's federal system was not a standard or perfect model of federalism. While such arguments were consistent for Laskin, Estey and McIntyre, who as dissenters had argued the same points on question two, they were a dramatic reversal for the "swing group" of judges.

Martland's and Ritchie's argument drew out the brazen nature of the double-barrelled federal contentions. The Canadian Parliament may pass *any* constitutional resolutions it likes; the United Kingdom *must* subsequently pass them. The dissenters rejected the first contention as an attack on the legally recognized federal principle and a "perversion" of Parliament's resolution procedures. In addition, they challenged the court majority's view that the absence of a clear prohibition against an action of this kind was sufficient to conclude that "the law knows nothing of any requirement of provincial consent." Instead, the dissenters insisted that the absence of a specific grant of power for such action, together with the express prohibition of any similar action by direct legislative enactment of Parliament under section 91 (1), suggested that the federal government's claims went too far.

With the September 28 judgement, Prime Minister Trudeau finally received an answer to an almost forgotten scholarly debate from the 1940s. In the end, the court had come down with an ingeniously split decision which Trudeau, Paul Gérin-Lajoie and the others in the debate could hardly have anticipated: seven to two that such a resolution was legal; six to three that it was improper and "unconstitutional." But the results were just as puzzling to non-specialists. The decision appeared to move in the direction of both parties and to settle nothing. But even if the decision was a split ruling, giving neither party a decisive win, the view that it settled nothing was quite wrong. It resolved two critical matters vital to everything that came afterward: *the resolution was legal* **and** *the resolution was constitutionally improper*. It would remain for the Canadian people and their legislatures and governments to see what value they placed upon legal power and principle respectively. It also remained to be seen what weight the country would give to national power and purpose on the one hand and regionalism and the federal principle on the other.

Hence, if the split decision is looked at from the perspective of statecraft, it must be acknowledged as artful. By giving each side a victory but neither a decisive win, the result constituted a virtual order to return to the bargaining table. Moreover, the rejection of unanimity had the effect of withdrawing blocking power from provincial hard-liners and of opening the way for a deal based on substantial agreement only. In refusing to define that measure more precisely, the court avoided the pitfalls of pronouncing on what was neither clear nor even required of it. Finally, the split ruling protected the court from the potentially dangerous political assault it would have faced had it decided wholly in favour of either bloc. It was not long before events bore out the political foresightedness of the court judgement.

# 5
# The Strategy of Agreement

The court decision tossed the issue back into the political arena, but not before it had shaped the terms of the ensuing struggle. On the one hand, it legalized federal unilateral action but stripped it of legitimacy; on the other hand, it threatened the provinces by removing any lingering doubts about the need for their unanimous consent to constitutional change affecting provincial powers. The pressure was immense for a return to negotiations and, though the atmosphere was still poisonous, events were forcing the governments towards a compromise deal where no single player could be a spoiler.

Before the implications of the court judgement had sunk in, the two sides began their usual jockeying. Justice Minister Chrétien waited scarcely a couple of hours before appearing before the nation to claim a federal victory on the grounds of legality. Forgetting entirely the broad grounds of justification for uni-lateral action that the federal government had been using for over a year, Chrétien claimed that the issue was strictly a matter of legality versus political convenience. The role of conventions was dismissed and the question of acting unconstitutionally even if legally was side-stepped entirely. It was an odd performance for a Canadian minister of justice. Dubbing Chrétien's posture as "legal trickery," opposition leader Joe Clark promised to fight the Liberals if they pushed on with the resolution in the face of the court's judgement.

The provinces decided to wait to hear Prime Minister Trudeau's reaction before responding to the decision. He did not speak until the evening of September 28 in a special broadcast from Seoul, South Korea, where he was paying a state visit. While Trudeau acknowledged the convention of provincial consent, he noted that after a half century of observance, it had frustrated efforts at patriation and could no longer be blindly followed. Unless there were signs of possible accommodation with the provinces, the message was clear: legal power rested with the federal government and it would "press on."

B.C. Premier William Bennett, who was acting as chairman of the eight provinces opposing the resolution, seized the olive branch reluctantly extended by Trudeau. He declared he would immediately visit all the premiers and would meet with the prime minister on his return to discuss the possibility of a further first ministers' conference. After correctly interpreting the court decision as an invitation to the political actors to resolve their differences, Bennett reiterated the premiers' view that the judgement had fully vindicated their contention that the resolution violated the constitution and the federal principle.

On October 3 the National Assembly of Quebec strengthened the hand of the Parti Québécois government by passing a resolution calling on the federal government to renounce unilateral action and to respect the conventions of the Canadian constitution. Most important, the resolution declared that the assembly "opposes every act which could interfere with its rights and affect its powers without its consent." The resolution passed 111 to 9 with all-party support. Federal leaders were upset that only nine provincial Liberals from predominantly anglophone ridings refused to join forces with the PQ.

Meanwhile, Blakeney and Bennett, the members of the Gang of Eight most inclined to compromise, were already signalling to Trudeau and Premier Davis of Ontario their conciliatory outlook. To them, Quebec's hard-line posture seemed unwise. Blakeney thought the Quebec assembly's action "premature," although Premier Lévesque argued that it did not go against the "essentials" of the dissident provinces' common front. Already members of the gang were beginning to move in opposite directions.

Lévesque's government, ignoring the dangers of isolating itself from the gang after the Supreme Court had appeared to give no province a veto, remained unyielding. There was constant talk of a Quebec referendum on federal unilateralism or even a national referendum to test whether the people supported Ottawa's package. The Quebec government also threatened to turn the PQ political machine onto the federal Liberals in Quebec. And while Lévesque upbraided Quebec MPs for their "incredible treachery" and "servility," the Quebec federal caucus responded with equal truculence and with a publicly paid $1 million advertising campaign to put its views to the Quebec people. The signs of an all-out political war between Quebec separatists and federalists were apparent.

Meanwhile on the broader federal-provincial front, political posturing went on among first ministers continents apart. Petty squabbles arose over who must offer the next compromise, whose timetable would be used, and who had the political muscle in Westminster. Trudeau had hoped to squeeze the Gang of Eight with an exceedingly tight timetable, a demand for compromises within the terms of his package and repeated threats to act unilaterally if the provinces did not comply. An angered Gang of Eight rejected Trudeau's position, demanded that he compromise on their Constitutional Accord of April 16, 1981, and on four separate occasions turned down Trudeau's calls to start talks. Both the preliminary meeting on October 13 between Trudeau and Bennett and later written exchanges between the dissenting premiers and the prime minister were unpleasant. Finally, following a premiers' meeting in Montreal on October 20 (which found premiers Davis and Hatfield asked to leave the meeting early), an invitation to meet was extended to Trudeau for the first week of November. He grudgingly accepted and set November 2 as a time for "one final attempt" to come to an agreement.

The dissident provinces had won the first round over timing. If they were to succeed at the negotiating table, however, they would need to agree on a minimum package acceptable to all sides. Although they publicly declared their April 16 accord to be that minimum, they all knew that they must be prepared to give further. But internal divisions made further movement as a bloc difficult. Thus, in private meetings, the premiers or their ministers failed to address a new "bottom-line position" and instead largely spent their time planning a strategy against any possible unilateral action.

For Lévesque and fellow hard-liner Sterling Lyon, the April accord was the negotiating minimum. Concerned about reports of separate exploratory talks between federal supporters and Saskatchewan and British Columbia, Lévesque hoped to put a stop to it by privately charging the moderates with betraying the group. But every premier knew there was little likelihood that the group could stay together once bargaining started in earnest. The real question was whether Lévesque and Lyon could keep the bloc together long enough to frustrate the prospects of an agreement satisfactory to the federal government. On the other hand, if the moderates could prevent the negotiations from becoming so polarized by offering concessions, the chances were much stronger that the hard-liners would be isolated and an agreement forged. Thus, although the appearance of federal-provincial conflict alone caught the public eye, the politics of interprovincial conflict was quietly being worked out within the "common front."

The moderates had by now realized that bargaining by a tough first-line "provincial consensus" ultimately played into the hands of the federal government. Although a provincial consensus was a·vital part of the bargaining — an indispensable first step — it could not be advanced inflexibly. That was the mistake made in the September 1980 talks. But the Gang of Eight could not compromise beyond their April 16 accord for reasons of basic political in-incompatibility.

For example, in the bargaining conducted largely through the media before the talks began, most members of the Gang of Eight had indicated a willingness to compromise on the Charter of Rights, as had the federal government. But, although most governments in English-speaking Canada were prepared to compromise to permit the entrenching of minority language educational rights, Quebec would not. And on this issue, as Premier Bennett sensed, the federal government would not move. There was no provincial consensus on this item (except for an entirely toothless "mini charter" allowing for provinces to opt in), despite its obvious importance. In the event of deadlock between the governments, Quebec on October 5 was already on record as favouring a referendum to settle the matter, while almost all the other provinces in the Gang of Eight were not. This difference remained unresolved. On the broader question of rights in the charter, the "common front" betrayed divisions between a premier like Lyon, who was unalterably opposed in principle, and a premier like Brian Peckford, who from the start was ready to support a charter. Even raising these issues would threaten their uneasy alliance.

Of course, at the root of unresolved differences, lay a fundamental incompatibility between the politics of committed federalists and a separatist premier of Quebec. Political differences could be glossed over in a common opposition to Ottawa's unilateral action, but once the business of federal renewal began they made unlikely partners. For Ontario, New Brunswick and the federal government, that was the most startling feature of the gang and they attributed its continuing at all to Lévesque's "duping" of the others. In its contacts with the moderates, Ontario reminded them of this incompatibility and of the fact that the PQ government could not afford to have a genuine compromise deal. It became part of the federal strategy to disengage the moderates from the bloc, to isolate

Quebec and reduce its influence over the others, and to secure a deal even if it had to exclude Quebec.

As the participants gathered in Ottawa on the Sunday evening prior to the First Ministers' Conference, each side prepared its position for the most sophisticated constitutional poker game since Confederation. But unlike September, 1980, there was more hope now for a negotiated solution. Public opinion demanded a settlement. Britain expected a consensus. The players themselves had only three (instead of twelve) items on the table. But most important, the requirement of unanimity was gone. Now, thanks to the Supreme Court, a deal could be concluded with "substantial" provincial consent only. Under these new conditions, the bargaining resembled a zero-sum game: not all players need be satisfied with an outcome and any outcome could advantage some at the expense of others. With the known divisions in the Gang of Eight, no province could be assured of not being odd man out if it proved inflexible.

On Monday, November 2, Trudeau opened the talks before a barrage of television cameras in the National Conference Centre. After citing the three topics to be settled — patriation, an amending formula and a Charter of Rights — he lost no time in seizing the initiative. The federal government was "flexible" on the amending formula though it preferred the Victoria formula and had reservations concerning "opting out" in the provincial accord formula, which it regarded as a form of "incremental separatism." On the Charter of Rights the government was ready to compromise on "timing and substance," but not on the principle. This staking out of the federal position with a generally conciliatory tone was important to assure the public of federal willingness to compromise and to strengthen the moderates' bargaining position within the Gang of Eight.

But the initiatives towards compromise did not end here. The federal government's provincial allies, premiers Davis of Ontario and Hatfield of New Brunswick, each proposed compromises on the two most contentious issues. Davis shifted dramatically toward the principles of the Gang of Eight by offering to give up an Ontario veto in the Victoria amending formula now in the federal resolution. This offer was a major concession. Not only was Ontario signalling its abstention from a claim to primacy on the grounds of population, but it was now virtually guaranteeing that the principle of formal constitutional equality among provinces might finally be adopted.

Hatfield offered an important compromise on the Charter of Rights. His proposal was to entrench most provisions of the charter, including those pertaining to language and education, but to hold in suspension the three sections that were most contentious as far as the provinces were concerned. As was seen in Chapter 2, these were the sections conferring legal and equality rights, together with the clause empowering citizens to get their rights enforced by the courts. Hatfield suggested that if, after a three-year delay, any six provinces continued to oppose these sections, they would become inoperable. This was the first concrete version of a limited charter which might overcome areas of contention and meet each side's minimum objectives. No other premiers spoke to the proposal in the public session, preferring, as one of them put it, "to poke at it with long sticks" before making any commitment. Hatfield's compromise was valuable in showing the kind of trade-off which an ally of the federal government thought necessary for success at the table: acceptance of the federal Liberals' bilingual program in return for a chance to delay and possibly defeat sections of the charter that most provinces found objectionable.

For the public part of the First Ministers' Conference, the Gang of Eight had decided to take a different tack. They used the occasion to lecture Ottawa for having attempted unilateral action and to underline their Supreme Court victory on the constitutional question. Although it dampened public expectations about their willingness to bargain, this strategy had several advantages. It preserved the common front; it signalled that the federal government would not get an agreement without significant concessions; it prepared the public for the complex battle over federalism which would follow if the talks broke down. The strategy permitted the provinces to confront the federal government directly for the first time in over a year and to express in the strongest terms their profound disagreement with the unconstitutional nature of federal actions.

Lévesque termed the federal resolution a "legal and political absurdity" and demanded that Trudeau seek an electoral mandate for unilateral action. Alberta Premier Peter Lougheed declared that the resolution "violates the spirit and intent of Confederation" and "flagrantly disregards our nation's history, traditions, and its principles." Lyon scolded Trudeau for sowing discord so deep that the federal system was prevented from tackling other urgent problems. And so it went. Although most moderates were less aggressive, they too reproached the government for violating federalism. Saskatchewan and British Columbia, however, went out of their way to declare themselves ready to compromise. And with unanimity "a ghost of conferences past," as Allan Blakeney pointed out, they had now from the Supreme Court "a whole new set of rules" and an "unparalleled opportunity to succeed."

The first afternoon of private bargaining was largely spent discussing the question of the amendment formula, with neither side giving any indication of what compromise might be acceptable. The Charter of Rights was not discussed until late afternoon, and the issue failed to isolate any members of the Gang of Eight in separate positions.

Tuesday, November 3, proved to be more fruitful, not because any agreements were actually reached, but because the way was prepared for an agreement. In the morning, the hard-liners Lévesque and Lyon tackled Trudeau in a bitter exchange that threatened chances of a deal. They appeared to be tempting a conference breakdown by drawing the players into personal antagonisms. At this point, Davis appealed to the other premiers to bargain in good faith, as they had promised in the public session, and offered to make the first move towards compromise. Provided compensation for opting out were dropped, Ontario would support the Gang of Eight's amending formula in return for its support for a modified Charter of Rights. This trading offer made explicit for the first time the linkage between the proposals of Davis and Hatfield the day before.

This deliberate swap had the desired effect. It permitted the players to put aside their differences over an amendment formula to see whether an accommodation over the charter could be worked out. This put pressure on the Gang of Eight at precisely the point where it was weakest. Premier Davis was deliberately vague on what kind of charter he had in mind, but Trudeau made clear that the charter on the table was contained in the current resolution as recently amended by Parliament.

In the afternoon, the Gang of Eight met with Premier Davis at the Chateau Laurier to discuss his compromise proposal and sent him to Prime Minister Trudeau across the street at the National Conference Centre to see whether he would entertain a proposal from the eight on the Charter of Rights. Trudeau agreed and premiers John Buchanan of Nova Scotia, Lougheed and Bennett were sent off bearing the group's "mini charter" proposal. Their offer was to defer most sections of the charter pending further study and to permit a provincial opting-in clause on minority language educational rights. This was the Gang of Eight's only united bargaining position on the charter, but it was unacceptable to the federal government. Trudeau lashed out at the premiers for bringing such a proposal, and suggested that they were being "duped" in their bargaining strategy by Quebec. Under no circumstances would the federal government give way on minority language educational rights.

When the Gang of Eight reassembled shortly afterward, it was clear that they were without a further common position on this critical matter. Premiers Blakeney and Bennett indicated that they had proposals of their own to make at the talks on the following morning. For Quebec, the long-feared break-up of the Gang of Eight seemed imminent, even though the premiers were still scrupulously abiding by the group's rules by giving "notice" of offering their own positions. Unless the group could coalesce around a new more substantial concession on the

Charter of Rights, the most moderate members would undo the alliance. All the earlier talk of secret bargaining among Saskatchewan, British Columbia and Ontario before the conference began to assume a more threatening form. A "chance" meeting of Ontario and Saskatchewan delegations at an Italian restaurant that evening did nothing to allay suspicions.

On Tuesday evening, the federal cabinet met in emergency session to consider its response to the Gang of Eight's amending formula and to consider final concessions over the charter. It was becoming clear that if a deal were to be struck, some give would be necessary on both items. At the same time, however, the federal side needed to examine its next strategic step carefully. If the momentum were to be retained and Ontario prevented from making a premature move towards the Gang of Eight, the referendum card on the Charter of Rights had to be played soon. By offering to put the Charter of Rights as well as the amending formula to a referendum if faced with deadlock in two years' time, the federal government knew that it could overcome any obstacles to its package in Britain and that it would force the provinces into a difficult political fight. But most important, it knew that the referendum proposal would split the Gang of Eight and isolate Quebec. Quebec was on record as supporting a referendum, while the English-speaking premiers regarded referenda as divisive. To federal strategists, these differences between Lévesque and the other premiers in the Gang of Eight could be exploited.

The following morning Saskatchewan tabled its compromise proposal for immediate entrenchment of all sections of the charter except for provincial "opting in" on legal and equality rights and for a non-enforceable declaration on minority language educational rights. Because this proposal did not fully protect minority language educational rights, the federal government could not accept it, nor were the other governments particularly enamoured with the compromise. None the less, Saskatchewan had started negotiations outside the terms of the provincial bloc of eight. For that reason, Quebec's minister of intergovernmental affairs, Claude Morin, in what he later described as a state of "consternation," angrily denounced Saskatchewan for departing from the "common front" principles. British Columbia meanwhile had that morning declared itself ready to accept the entrenchment of minority language educational rights.

In the presence of these divisions Trudeau introduced again his referendum card. Lévesque, losing confidence in the Gang of Eight's ability to stick to its principles, accepted Trudeau's challenge. After only the most general discussion of the referendum proposal on the Wednesday morning's closed-door session, Lévesque and Trudeau appeared before the television cameras. These arch-rivals had now apparently agreed on a referendum to settle their differences if a negotiated settlement proved impossible. Lévesque was confident that he could defeat a referendum on a Charter of Rights and, in any event, he was willing to let the decision be made by the people after extensive debate. If the April accord were to be abandoned, a referendum seemed a surer defence of Quebec's interests.

Premier Lougheed and virtually all the other English-speaking premiers were offended by the idea of a referendum and were shaken by Quebec's violation of the gang's principles. While Saskatchewan had given advance notice of its compromise proposal, Quebec had given the other premiers no notice of its lining up with Trudeau on a referendum. This move presented them with a clear threat if they could not come up with a negotiated settlement. Premier Lévesque in this respect misjudged the extent to which most premiers in the group wanted a settlement to avoid public wrath at home, ongoing national divisiveness and the embarrassment of a public brawl in Britain.

The referendum option was seen to be a trap by Lévesque only after he belatedly learned the implementation details of the federal proposal. In a paper tabled in the afternoon session, Trudeau offered him a referendum only if, after enactment by Westminster, all provinces agreed to have one. Without such agreement, Trudeau's proposals would apply as law. Lévesque began to pull back, complaining to the other premiers and the public that the federal referendum details were unacceptable. But it was too late. The damage to his earlier alliance was already done and Quebec's ability to contain events severely circumscribed.

From Trudeau's perspective, the referendum idea worked either as a bargaining lever or as an acceptable method, after two further years of talks, of breaking federal-provincial deadlock. The irony of the situation was that his tactic enjoyed the support of his archrivals in Quebec, even though it threatened them above all others. Closing Wednesday's full meeting with a promise to work on the referendum details over which Quebec took exception, Trudeau kept pressure on the players. Unless there was some change, all of them would face a fractious referendum debate and public contempt for yet another failure to compromise.

Faced with those conditions and only one more day of talks, a deal was put together that night giving the dissenting provinces their amending formula (minus the section providing for intergovernmental delegating of powers and Quebec's demand for financial compensation for "opting out"), and the federal government a limited Charter of Rights. The essential strength of the bloc trading strategy was therefore borne out, even though massive public pressure for a compromise including the Charter of Rights played a crucial role in getting an agreement.

The six moderates among the Gang of Eight, this time led by Premier Peckford of Newfoundland, decided to accept the entrenchment of minority language rights for each of their provinces. In return they demanded a "notwithstanding clause" — the right to legislate so as to expressly override certain sections of the charter whenever their legislatures might think it necessary to do so. This was the essential bargain struck. In many respects, it was the compromise towards which the parties had been painstakingly moving all week, if not for a month before the talks had started: acceptance of the key federal interest in the charter in return for accommodating the opposition of the English-speaking provinces to entrenchment as a method of protecting rights. As fortune would have it, the deal was accomplished without the attendance of the two hard-liners among the Gang of Eight. Manitoba's Sterling Lyon was forced to depart from the conference early to resume electioneering in an unsuccessful bid to retain power. Quebec's René Lévesque, who was now thought to prefer a referendum to any such compromise, was not invited to participate.

The negotiations had been conducted between two groups: premiers and representatives from six provinces meeting in Saskatchewan's suite on the Peckford proposal and a group of key ministers and aides — Jean Chrétien, Michael Kirby, Roy Romanow, and Ontario attorney general Roy McMurtry (and later Premier Davis himself) — meeting on their own to see what kind of compromise might save the conference. Among other matters, they agreed to qualify the mobility rights section to allow for affirmative action programs in provinces with low employment and to drop aboriginal treaty rights, reportedly on the insistence of Alberta and British Columbia. After the main lines had been settled, spokesmen from both Prince Edward Island and Alberta conferred with Manitoba's ministers to bring that province into the accord. Premier Lyon agreed on condition that Manitoba's legislature later approve the minority language education provision. Ontario used its influence with the federal government to convince it to go along. Premier Hatfield could be expected to agree especially since entrenched minority language rights were part of the package. Only Quebec's participation was in doubt as the final parts of the deal were concluded around 4:00 Thursday morning. It was not until the regular breakfast meeting of the old Gang of Eight that Premier Lévesque learned of the full compromise which had been worked out without him.

Confronted with a *fait accompli*, Lévesque felt blackmailed. He was happy neither with the deletion of the fiscal compensation feature of the original provinces' accord, nor with the wording of the mobility rights section.

When the full meeting reconvened later in the morning, Trudeau asked Peckford to summarize the new proposal and then heard every premier speak on it. All but Quebec assented. Trudeau then finally showed his hand by declaring that he felt there was "common ground." He asked however for three important changes to the agreement.

● He requested that the last sentence in section 3 (c) be struck. The section read as follows:

> We have agreed that the provisions of Section 23 in respect of Minority Language Education Rights will apply to our Provinces. Any Province not agreeing to be bound by this Section continues to have the right to accept the application of the Section to their Province at any future time.

By securing the deletion of the last sentence, Trudeau removed any suggestion of Quebec retaining the right to opt out of the minority language educational guarantees.

● He asked that a sunset provision be put on the use of "notwithstanding clauses." Thus, if any government made use of the right to legislate against fundamental freedoms or legal and equality rights, the limitations would lapse after a five-year period unless re-enacted by that legislature. This change was designed to put the responsibility for acting against the charter on each government and to make it face regularly the political consequences of continuing to act against it.

● Finally, he asked that the subject of aboriginal rights be put on the agenda of a future first ministers' constitutional conference and that representatives of the aboriginal peoples of Canada be invited to participate in that discussion. This suggestion, which reconfirmed one of the promises made to native peoples in the earlier resolution, was accepted. In this way, Trudeau tried to soften the impact of the ignoble deletion of aboriginal treaty rights.

As for Quebec, Trudeau did not agree to consider its demands that financial compensation be provided a province which opted out of amendments to the constitution or that the mobility rights section be rewritten. To guarantee compensation to any province, Trudeau asserted, would invite the wealthier provinces to opt out of all amendments that imposed a heavy financial burden on the central government. Even though Lévesque hinted that he might go along with the minority language educational guarantees if these two demands were met, Trudeau did not take up either suggestion. He only promised to consider Quebec's case later. Perhaps fearful that the package would unravel if Quebec's demands again were entertained at the eleventh hour, and conscious that a firm deal was in hand, Trudeau decided not to risk all in an effort to bring Quebec in. Besides, by forcing Lévesque to go before the people with limited objections to the deal, Trudeau deprived the Quebec premier of the broadest grounds of political opposition which might otherwise have been effective in Quebec. Trudeau knew too that he could later offer substantial concessions to Lévesque and hence politically box him in. As the first ministers returned to face the cameras, it was clear who had suffered most by the court's rejection of the unanimity rule. Once again alone, once again odd man out, Quebec, Lévesque declared, stood abandoned by its anglophone partners in the Gang of Eight, an unwilling victim of an apparently correct constitutional procedure. As the others celebrated, a bitter Lévesque warned that the consequences would be "incalculable."

The conference bargaining was over. An agreement had been forged between nine provinces and the federal government. But the debate over the subject was just beginning. With Quebec out of the deal it was clear that the acrimony between the Quebec government and Ottawa would go on. Moreover, the settlement could be presented in Quebec as a defeat of the province's interests, creating yet further instability in the relationship between that province and the rest of Canada. This time the dispute was not confined to a PQ-Ottawa feud, but had escalated into a fundamental collision between the PQ government and all other governments in Canada. Now the bonds of "friendliness and understanding" which had, according to Claude Morin, developed between the Quebec government and the other provincial governments appeared to be severed. It was, from the point of view of the Quebec government, a "deplorable and painful" conclusion to a unique interprovincial enterprise.

At the same time, from the perspective of the other participants the conference had to be reckoned a success, even if the exclusion of Quebec made it a less than complete one. The other governments had finally agreed on a package of constitutional changes which, even if it did not fully satisfy each, achieved what none before them had been able to secure: patriation, an amending formula, a Charter of Rights and several other important changes. Most of them did not accept the Parti Québécois charge that the other governments had "misled" and "abandoned" Quebec.

The PQ government subsequently declared that it was betrayed when, during the negotiations on the

Wednesday, the other members in the Gang of Eight began to leave the interprovincial common front and put forth alternative propositions, developed without Quebec, and when Quebec's delegation was left out of the crucial compromise discussions that night. According to Claude Morin, the April 16 accord was "a real contract" which could not be unilaterally modified in order to find a negotiated solution with Ottawa. Yet if a negotiated settlement with Ottawa was to be achieved, further movement from the premiers' April 16 accord was unavoidable, as Quebec's government well knew. Indeed, Quebec had received notice from Saskatchewan about its readiness to propose a separate compromise, and it had known for at least a month before the talks began that several members of the gang were publicly indicating their willingness to compromise beyond the accord.

If a negotiated settlement were to be pursued then, the April 16 provincial accord would be on the table for discussion just as would the Charter of Rights and other proposals of the federal government, Ontario and New Brunswick. Since the gang had no coherent collective compromises to put into play in the negotiations, it was obvious that members who wanted a settlement would eventually have to float their own proposals or face a breakdown in the talks. Once the federal side had virtually conceded to the gang's amending formula, the pressure was intense on the dissenting premiers to come up with a compromise over the charter. Yet no sooner had they begun to do so, than the Quebec government broke ranks and accepted the federal government's referendum offer. This action freed the hands of those premiers who were ready to compromise.

Thus it might be more reasonable to see Quebec's dilemma at the bargaining table as stemming not from "betrayal" but from the impossibly difficult situation in which the PQ government was placed. Its deepest commitment lay not in renewing federalism but in dismantling it; yet Quebecers had empowered the government to pursue federalism only. Success at the bargaining table would undermine the Parti Québécois's argument that federalism does not work, set back the independence movement and imperil the government's position with its party base. Therefore its fundamental political interest lay in continuing federal-provincial conflict, in goading the federal government into more arrogant displays of unilateralism and in preserving a bloc of provincial opposition. To advance such objectives, the PQ government had signed the April 1981 accord, tactically conceding its veto in return for a right to opt out with compensation; when faced with negotiations in which members of the gang began to show signs of compromising with the federal government, Lévesque seized the first opportunity which Trudeau extended to him to avert that danger by preserving on-going conflict in a final referendum battle over the Charter of Rights. Yet nothing could have been better calculated to push the other premiers into a final negotiated compromise with Ottawa.

## The Return of Public Participation: Women's and Native Rights

It took less than two weeks for Parliament to debate the new constitutional resolution. It was passed with all-party agreement on December 2, 1981. Though amendments to give Quebec full compensation for opting out, to strengthen the rights of Quebec's anglophone minority and to protect the rights of the unborn were attempted, none were successful. The Senate, after turning back similar amendments, including one which would have restored the Senate veto over constitutional changes, confirmed the package on December 8 and the resolution was immediately dispatched to Great Britain. That rapid turnaround after more than a year of wrangling was possible chiefly because the resolution, whatever its merit, now appeared to carry constitutional legitimacy. Nine provinces and the federal government had sanctioned it — probably enough intergovernmental agreement to meet the Supreme Court's test for "substantial [not unanimous] provincial consent." This political achievement also stemmed from the relative open-mindedness and flexibility which the federal government showed to most criticism of the new constitution. Since the deal was not entirely of its making, it was easy to agree with public and opposition criticism that it did not go far enough and to blame that result on the hazards of negotiations. The government had preferred a stronger charter but had been pressured into bargaining over clauses in exchange for federal-provincial consensus; if the results were not to everyone's liking, that was manifestly *not* the government's fault. The accord would be honoured, unless nine provincial premiers could be persuaded to amend its terms to meet public disappointments.

The notwithstanding clause permitting provinces to override certain sections of the Charter of Rights came in for the most general criticism; women's groups in particular decided to do battle to have the clause removed from section 28 of the resolution, which enshrined equality between men and women. Even though such a result ironically might threaten the effectiveness of affirmative action programs for women by making it easier for *men* to use section 28 against such legislation, strengthening section 28 became a cause célèbre for women's rights. The federal government declared itself ready to make that change, if provincial consent could be obtained. A national lobby campaign began to influence provincial governments. One by one premiers caved in to public pressure until only Premier Blakeney of Saskatchewan remained opposed. He declared Saskatchewan ready to comply only if native treaty rights were also restored.

This linkage between the grievances of both groups was a timely suggestion. Ever since the accord had been announced, native peoples had expressed disgust at the deletion of their treaty rights from the constitutional package. They too had begun a campaign to see their treaty rights restored. The federal government was ready to do so, although it reminded native peoples that some native groups had actively opposed the earlier resolution. Pressure in Parliament, especially from the New Democratic Party, and the steady pressure of native groups and public opinion brought the premiers around, particularly after Blakeney had stated his position. By November 26, Parliament had unanimously restored both sections, although the word "existing" was attached to the definition of aboriginal treaty rights, an addition that left native peoples uneasy.

This second entry of public interest groups into the constitutional struggle was fully as interesting and important as the first. Two of the same interest groups (particularly the women's associations) that had pressed for changes in the federal resolution in the fall of 1980 now converted themselves into a national lobby to make the governmental players respect the rights they had won earlier. Since Ottawa had already been convinced, the new targets were the provincial governments. To bring pressure to bear in all the provincial capitals required the combination of active local associations, a vigorous national campaign and relentless media exposure. It was too much for the premiers to withstand.

Apart from the commitment of the organizations' many supporters, the success of the campaign owed a good deal to the broad popularity of the federal charter and the strategic support which the federal government gave its "allies." At this critical point the government extended assistance through Mines Minister Judy Erola (who was responsible for women's issues in cabinet) and it joined with opposition spokesmen in promoting the idea of limited changes. While promising to stick to the terms of the agreement unless changes were consented to by the premiers, Ottawa quietly relished the discomfort which the provincial governments faced from an outraged public. It was no secret that the greatest glee was reserved for Allan Blakeney's government which, in the view of the federal government, had played a crafty and self-satisfied role through the whole constitutional struggle.

Hence, federally sponsored public participation took the lines which planners expected. There was no serious assault upon the essentials of the intergovernmental bargain; though disappointment surfaced over the notwithstanding clause in the charter, there was no concerted attempt to have it removed. In that sense, the public groups focused on more limited matters and tacitly bowed to the outcome of the governmental bargaining.

The role of public participation throughout the constitutional struggle, therefore, was not a one-dimensional "people versus governments" conflict. Although it often flattered public interest groups to think so, and it suited the federal government to paint the struggle in that way, in fact public participation almost always had the stamp of federal management on it. That fact was obvious in the Kirby memorandum's plan for orchestrating public opinion around the clashing themes of "people's rights versus provincial powers"; it was evident in the careful selection, management and wooing of public interest groups in the Joint Parliamentary Committee; and it was apparent in the unleashing of these groups upon the premiers after intergovernmental agreement on the constitution had been achieved. Of course, the strategy did depend on genuine public enthusiasm for a Charter of Rights, but there is no doubt that public participation was carefully channelled into the federal battle against provincial claims and powers. Whenever public participation did not comply with federal requirements — such as with the ill-fated opposition of aboriginal peoples to patriation itself — it was firmly blocked with the full political and legal powers of the central government.

The reason for the selective federal cultivation of the public in its constitutional plans went well beyond the political needs of the moment. The federal argument for amendment by referenda and for the charter had reflected carefully prepared efforts to block growing provincial power by working out a direct alliance between the federal government/Parliament/courts and the Canadian people. The referendum proposals in particular sought to build a new constitutional alignment between the national government and the "people" as the prime constituents of Canadian federalism; the charter sought to tie the people both practically and symbolically to a new constitutional system enshrining rights from coast to coast. Such a sophisticated strategy, reinforced by aggressive federal unilateralism in many areas of public policy, was designed to undercut what Ottawa considered a dangerous advance of provincial power under the mantle of regionalism.

## Strategic Fallout in Quebec

This plan was particularly designed for Quebec. Out-manoeuvring the Parti Québécois government and securing a package of constitutional reform which would win over Quebecers to Canada was always the chief objective of the federal government. Since it was considered axiomatic that Lévesque's government could not be a party to any such deal, it was the aim of federal strategists to win over the people of Quebec and hence to isolate the separatists. For its part, the PQ government was determined to identify its case with that of the Quebec people so that, if it could not accede to a deal, it would be said that Quebec as a whole had been betrayed. Hence, the irony that without separatist endorsement of federal renewal, the province of Quebec was outside the deal — a stain upon the historic accord of November 5. It was in this strange setting that Quebec's federal and provincial leaders — diehard federalists and separatists alike — sought to voice Quebecers' split political loyalties. Where Quebecers actually stood was unclear.

Lévesque, outside the agreement, tried to give full

vent to what he hoped would be his people's sense of isolation and anger. Quebec, he declared, would not accept federal overtures to talk over remaining differences and would not participate in future federal-provincial conferences except when they concerned its vital financial interests. Lévesque spurned Trudeau's belated offers to consider compensation for opting out in education and cultural matters in the amending formula, to rewrite the mobility rights section provided other provinces agreed, and to refrain from imposing on Quebec minority language educational guarantees for immigrants. In the end, Trudeau put most of these protections into the resolution on his own (with support from the other premiers) and took upon himself the mantle of Quebec's protector.

Rarely had the rhetoric of Quebec politicians become as vituperative as it then did. Federal leaders were branded as "whores" and "traitors," while Quebec itself was pictured as the innocent victim of rapists. On the subject of Quebec's loss of veto, Trudeau in turn acidly remarked that the province lost out at the April 81 premiers' conference when Lévesque "left [the veto] at the door with his galoshes."

There was no disguising that Lévesque was politically boxed in. Polls suggested that he could not win the support of the Quebec people either in a referendum or snap election. Nor could he win all-party support for a resolution in the Quebec assembly; even Claude Ryan, unhappy with the deal, could not support the Parti Québécois further. In vain, Lévesque demanded recognition of a Quebec veto and acceptance of the principle of "national self-determination." The Quebec government finally decided to issue a formal veto against the constitutional resolution, an action which the Supreme Court appeared to have rendered legally redundant; it also referred the question of the alleged violation of Quebec's veto to its Court of Appeal. But neither of these initiatives could now block the way to patriation.

It appeared that Ottawa had won at the bargaining table and in the immediate battle for public opinion. Indeed, Lévesque became so enraged over the federal manoeuvres that he threatened to run on an outright separatist plank in the next Quebec election, a sudden shift from his government's formal sovereignty-association platform and one he later recanted. But his invective stirred up the hard-liners, which contributed to a collision between the government and party delegates over the strategy for Quebec independence in a convention in Montreal on the weekend of December 5. Despite the pleas of the premier and most ministers, the delegates vented their anger with English Canada by voting to drop "association" from the party's platform and to push for unqualified sovereignty. The cabinet only retrieved itself from the embarrassing spectacle by demanding a vote of the full party with Lévesque's own resignation hanging in the balance if the vote went against him. And even before the results of the mail ballot supporting Lévesque had come in, Claude Morin, the PQ's experienced minister of intergovernmental affairs and architect of Quebec's ill-fated negotiating policy, had tendered his resignation. His departure alone signalled that the Quebec government's position was weakening.

Yet whether the results in the long term will advance the federalist cause in Quebec is quite debatable. Although the winning of minority language educational rights for French-speaking citizens in all the other provinces does constitute an important victory for the idea of Canada, rather than Quebec, as the French Canadian homeland, there is little doubt that, apart from the section on natural resources, the new Canadian constitution does not add but rather subtracts from the powers of the Quebec legislature. In that respect, the deal can only be a setback for the vast majority of Quebecers who had associated constitutional renewal with increased Quebec powers. Moreover, it is unclear to what extent the winning of French rights throughout Canada can compensate for a reduction in Quebec's own powers. In effect, the federal gamble is that Quebecers will opt for a national expansion of their linguistic and cultural rights over the traditional "defence of the homeland" posture. Whether Quebecers will swap ethnic nationalism for Trudeau's pluralistic liberal substitute remains to be seen.

What can be said with certainty is that the new Canadian constitution did not end the row between francophone elites over the role and status of Quebec and Quebecers in Canada. Not only did it not settle that dispute, the constitution actually provides the battleground for a second critical confrontation between Quebec separatists and federalists. In the wake of the constitutional settlement, the Parti Québécois was gearing up for an unprecedented electoral challenge to the federal Liberals in the next national election, and had committed itself to run on a stronger sovereignty plank (with merely an offer of association with English Canada) in the next Quebec election. Against it the federal Liberals hold out to Quebecers the enshrinement of French language rights throughout Canada and any other offers of constitutional change which public opinion may indicate are needed to ensure most Quebecers' loyalty to the "Canada first" option. Since the amending formula is flexible, changes will be much more easily accomplished, especially those that *add* to provincial powers or specifically concede additional powers to Quebec.

Thus the new Canadian constitution marks an important stage in the continuing battle for Quebecers' allegiance. The politics of competing homelands will go on with as yet no indication of the ultimate victor in this struggle. The outcome of the November, 1981, negotiations can easily be presented as a clear defeat of Quebec's interest. Not only can it be said that the constitution was imposed by majority anglophone governments on Quebec without its consent, but the provisions will be attacked for reducing Quebec's powers and for giving expression only to the arbitrary vision of Pierre Elliott Trudeau. These criticisms may be persuasive since the Quebec referendum certainly did not give Trudeau and the federal Liberals a mandate to impose the new constitution upon Quebec. But with Quebecers themselves having backed these two irreconcilable elites and instructed them to pursue federal renewal, no happier results could reasonably have been expected. Hence, for as long as most Quebecers remain divided over how they should exist as a people, the "homelands debate" will remain with them and all other Canadians.

# 6
# The New Canadian Constitution

With the achievement of substantial federal-provincial agreement over the new Canadian constitution, the political turbulence which the Canada Act had generated in Britain largely passed away. The central battle over unilateral action was over. As the formerly dissenting premiers mothballed their meticulous battleplans for a propaganda war in Britain, Westminster looked forward to a relatively easy passage. Although the opposition of the government of Quebec and of Canadian native peoples certainly was a matter of regret, it did not present Britain with anything like the serious political and constitutional difficulties it would have faced from federal unilateral action. The news of an agreement was therefore received at Westminster with relief.

Although Quebec's lobbying in Britain continued and on December 19, 1981, an appeal was made to the British government to delay action until Canadian courts had finally pronounced on the matter of a Quebec veto, Westminister saw little reason for further delay. The legal and conventional requirements set out by the Canadian Supreme Court for requesting patriation and other changes appeared to have been fully met. Even Sir Anthony Kershaw, who had chaired the committee studying Britain's responsibility on the question, now agreed that Westminster should act swiftly in accordance with the request.

Native peoples also continued their opposition in Great Britain. They won sympathy for their cause, but, since the issue of native rights was regarded as an internal Canadian matter, Westminster could not change the resolution without trespassing on Canadian sovereignty. Native peoples challenged the proposition that jurisdiction over Indians had been totally transferred to the Parliament of Canada by arguing before the British Court of Appeal that the British crown retained responsibility for Canada's native peoples, but the court on January 28 unanimously rejected the contention. A request to appeal the matter to the House of Lords was denied.

As the Canada Act proceeded through the required legislative stages, some members of the Commons and House of Lords continued to voice concern over Quebec's dissent and over the opposition of native peoples, but at no time did these objections seriously threaten passage. On March 8 the Canada Act received final approval in the British House of Commons and, on March 25, the endorsement of the House of Lords. Four days later the queen assented to the Canada Act. The only remaining formality was the proclamation or bringing into force of the act; at the request of the Canadian government, the queen agreed to come to Canada to proclaim the new constitution on April 17.

If the process of approval at Westminster was quicker and smoother than participants could have thought possible only a year before, many Canadians still had doubts about the advisability of proceeding with the Canada Act prior to court judgements over Quebec's right of veto. Though the Supreme Court decision appeared to have weakened *any* province's case for a veto, it was still unclear whether Quebec might not constitute a special case. Many constitutional specialists were by no means certain that Quebec did not have a powerful argument. But on April 7 the Quebec Court of Appeal delivered a unanimous decision rejecting Quebec's claim to a veto. It ruled that the constitutional agreement reached on November 5 by Ottawa and nine provinces satisfied the Supreme Court's requirement of "substantial provincial consent," and that all provinces were on an equal footing under the constitution. Both the force of the strongly worded legal opinion and the fact that it was unanimous appeared to sanction the position that the British and Canadian governments had taken. Planning for the proclamation on April 17 continued, undeterred by Premier Lévesque's announcement that he would appeal to the Supreme Court of Canada. Although a reversal by the higher court was always possible, it seemed to federal attorneys a very unlikely outcome.

## Patriation

After two days of celebration in Ottawa following the queen's arrival on April 15, proclamation day arrived. The signing was carried out on a special platform on Parliament Hill before a nation-wide television audience. Three prominent Quebecers affixed their signatures to the proclamation signed by the queen —Trudeau, Chrétien, and André Ouellet, minister of consumer and corporate affairs and registrar-general — while thousands of dissenters in Quebec gathered in Montreal to hear the constitution denounced by

Premier Lévesque. Federal leaders from Quebec could take comfort from polls showing that most Quebecers who had an opinion wanted the province to sign the agreement, but the protests in Montreal, as well as those quietly staged by native peoples, were still unpleasant reminders of opposition to this form of national renewal.

Patriation then was not to be achieved without resistance. Yet the protests did not disguise the fact that the country was undergoing an important transformation. While Britain's ceding of legal power over Canada's constitution was on one level a purely ceremonial act confirming an independence spanning at least a half century, on another level, it symbolized a certain spiritual coming of age for Canadians. With Britain no longer a trustee, no longer able to provide a final outside check against Canadians having to live together under their own rules, the country was now alone and freer to become what it would be. And although historical grievances from Quebec or from the Western and Atlantic provinces did appear to legitimize suspicions and the need for an outside umpire, patriation challenged Canadians to go beyond past injuries and to structure an independent future.

It was also not coincidental that while the constitutional battle to cut remaining legal ties with the United Kingdom was underway, initiatives were simultaneously being made to increase Canadian control of the economy. The National Energy Program, which aimed to "Canadianize" the oil and gas industry, was another part of the Liberal "new nationalism" which sought to come to grips with accumulated weaknesses in the Canadian state. In fact Ottawa's unilateral constitutional initiative had only preceded the introduction of the National Energy Program into Parliament by approximately two weeks. It is therefore natural to see the federal drive for patriation in the context of a wider national program for independence presided over by a strengthened federal government.

## Canadian Charter of Rights and Freedoms

But the most popular part of the Canada Act for the Canadian citizen was probably the Charter of Rights. Now part of Canada's fundamental law, it compares well with rights charters in other countries and surpasses by far earlier bills of rights or previous draft charters. It takes a giant step beyond the Canadian Bill of Rights passed in 1960 during the prime ministership of John Diefenbaker. The Diefenbaker bill was a statute applying to the federal level of government only, and its rights provisions were not nearly as comprehensive nor its purpose in overriding other federal enactments as clear as the charter's. Unlike the Bill of Rights, the charter is "entrenched" and may not simply be abrogated by statutory declaration of any future Parliament. It moves well beyond what was achieved in the 1971 Victoria Conference by covering areas which had been completely gutted at that time — especially legal, equality and minority language educational rights. This is true even if there has been a fall back in the establishment of French language access at provincial legislative and administrative levels. The new provisions on mobility and native rights are valuable improvements over earlier draft charters.

Many of the improvements in the charter arise directly from the role played by public interest groups during the constitutional struggle. In part, too, they are the product of the unusually diligent work of the

Joint Parliamentary Committee. But most significant of all, a strong charter was the product of the convergence of public concern with the national interests and strategy of the federal government.

Examples of a "citizens'-first" approach can be seen in many drafting changes but most particularly in the demand that any limits to Canadians' rights be "reasonable" and that the onus for justifying any limits be placed directly upon governments. Section 1 puts the burden of proof on the would-be suppressor of rights to "demonstrably justify" restrictions upon freedoms. This clause, which provides unavoidable discretionary power to the courts, will test the Supreme Court's philosophy over human rights and public order. Although the relative toughness and precision of the current wording should work in the citizen's favour, what the courts may in the future think are "reasonable" restrictions upon Canadians' freedoms simply cannot be known in advance. It is possible, for example, that unusually high provincial standards for practising certain professions may be struck down as "unreasonable" restrictions upon Canadians' rights to move and take up employment anywhere in the country. Many provincial and federal laws may be assailed for "unreasonable" discrimination in violation of the right to equality under section 15. Laws regulating pornography may also be successfully attacked for placing "unreasonable" restrictions upon freedom of expression.

An effect of the charter that seemed largely unnoticed was the open invitation it holds out for the establishment of affirmative action programs. Under section 6(4), constitutional recognition is accorded programs to ameliorate social and economic disparities, while under section 15(2) the same recognition is extended to programs to improve conditions for specially disadvantaged individuals and groups. While the legal aim of each of these sections was simply to permit governments to pursue such programs without other entrenched rights presenting a constitutional barrier, the indirect moral and political effects of constitutional recognition may be considerable. Certainly it will be easier to mount and justify such programs in the light of these provisions. In that respect, however, women may discover that section 28 guaranteeing equal rights to men and women, which they fought to have strengthened, will stand in the way of affirmative action programs on their behalf precisely because they violate such equality. By removing section 28 from the scope of the notwithstanding clause (section 33), and by making section 15(2) subject to section 28, women may have unwittingly disqualified themselves from the benefits of such affirmative action programs.

The much-criticized legislative override (clause 33), which permits provincial legislatures or Parliament to legislate against certain rights by expressly declaring that laws shall operate *notwithstanding* the charter's provisions, is a more defensible political alternative than the limitation clause in the Victoria Charter. The Victoria Charter permitted governments to limit rights whenever "public safety, order, health or morals, . . . national security, or the rights and freedoms of others" were involved. That was virtually an invitation to judicial caution. With the legislative recourse to a notwithstanding clause, the courts should not feel constrained to accept limits on rights whenever the legislatures have not expressly declared otherwise. Therefore if it be one of the objects of an entrenched charter to prod the courts into a more activist defence of citizens' rights, the 1981 Charter of Rights and Freedoms may be a far more aptly drafted document than any of its predecessors.

The possible impact of the notwithstanding clause upon court treatment of rights cases only underlines the need to avoid simplistic responses to the charter. The actual effects which a constitutional Charter of Rights may have can never be gleaned from looking merely at the text. Apart from the obvious fact that the words may not always mean the same thing to all persons, especially as they are actually applied in divergent circumstances, the legal players in the court-room process represent crucial factors. The legislative will reflected in the charter must be filtered through a judicial system of lawyers and judges where, almost by definition, the values and biases of the legal profession will necessarily predominate.

As the eminent professor of political science Donald Smiley has argued, neither the conservative predisposition of the legal profession nor its narrowly based educational training is likely to produce the most informed and generous interpretation of rights under the charter. It is generally conceded that, if any-thing, the Canadian legal profession tends to be more cautious and conservative than its American counter-part, and yet it is principally to legal practitioners that we have entrusted the interpretation of our entrenched rights and freedoms. Narrowness is further reinforced by the restricted character of court membership. The composition of the Supreme Court is not remotely "representative" of the nation — women, for example, who comprise over half the population only won a seat on it in 1982. In view of these facts, and of the longer history of conservative judgements by the Supreme Court in the United States, Canadians may come to regard the legislative override in section 33 not as a lamentable loophole, conceded to provincial premiers at the people's expense, but as a valuable democratic check upon conservative court decisions.

Constitutional specialists like Trudeau himself, who came to maturity during the heady days of American legal reform under Chief Justice Earl Warren, tend to forget that the Supreme Court in the United States was anything but a champion of human rights for most of its history. Consider, for example, the blacks' struggle for legal recognition. Constitutional guarantees in the Fourteenth Amendment did not protect blacks from segregation, until a liberal court finally upset earlier precedents in 1954. Constitutionally entrenched guarantees were equally powerless to prevent repression of political radicals on many occasions, as well as to spare Japanese Americans the pitiful treatment they received during the Second World War. Those "progressives" with selective memories also tend to forget that the absence of court vigilance in defence of human rights constitutes only part of the Supreme Court's history of conservatism. Not only did the court not interpret civil rights provisions on behalf of those for whom they were intended, it often used them to protect big business and other special interest groups against state regulation for the public good.

Assorted rights, especially in the Fifth and Fourteenth Amendments of the United States Constitution, were used by the Supreme Court to invalidate laws protecting the general public from exploitative labour practices. Laws regulating hours of work, minimum wage laws, labour conditions for women and even those banning child labour were successfully struck down by a Supreme Court more intent on protecting

vested property interests than broader human rights.
Not even the introduction of an income tax law got by
the court successfully until many years of pressure
forced conservative justices to reverse themselves. So
thoroughly reactionary had the court become in its
aggressive counter-attack on the New Deal in the
1930s that President Roosevelt had to initiate a measure to pack the court with his own nominees before
it reversed itself and accepted the beginnings of the
welfare state. Such a history of political and ideologi-
cal struggle in the United States ought at least to warn
Canadians not to be naïve about the mystique of
judicial neutrality and objectivity.

Of course it also does not follow that when the
American Supreme Court has been more liberal and
activist, its decisions have always been in keeping with
the public good. Consider the dubious value of court-
ordered bussing for example or the excessively liberal
injunctions against regulating everything from pornography to bulletin boards. While it is undeniable that
since the 1950s important strides have been made in
judicial protection of civil rights — especially in
combatting racial discrimination and providing
Americans with legal rights against arbitrary police
procedures — it would be myopic to associate such
libertarianism with supreme courts as such.

The least that Canadians can expect from their new
Charter of Rights is a spate of cases testing the Canadian Supreme Court's political leaning and vigilance
on many fundamental matters of social value, including abortion, capital punishment, sexual equality and
so on. On the basis of past experience, Canadians
have no reason to expect startling results. By training
and philosophy our judges will be much less inclined
to be activist than their American counterparts. But

whatever they do, judges will run a much heavier risk of being seen to be political than ever before. The pressure of public expectations will weigh heavily upon them and the threat of public censure will be an unavoidable part of their work.

As the courts become transformed, so too will Canadian society and politics. Many political conflicts now fought out in legislative chambers or meeting halls will increasingly become legal matters. Citizens groups may well channel their attention to the court-room — hiring batteries of lawyers to advance their political interests against other individuals, groups or governments.

The notwithstanding clause, however, provides a political escape-hatch from the results of the litigious process. Such a mechanism is a boon both to the courts and to democratic principles. It removes from the courts the ultimate responsibility for defining many of our values with only the cumbersome procedure of constitutional amendment as a check; it upholds democratic principles by restoring the right to make final choices to the people themselves. If that right is sometimes exercised unwisely, that is, one might reply, the necessary price of politics, a price we would be required to pay even if the political choices were to devolve upon nine judicial sages in Ottawa.

It is perhaps unfortunate that in the long constitutional debate this democratic principle was so often equated with "Parliamentary sovereignty." That suited the political interests and rhetoric of so many anglophone Conservative premiers and traditionalists, but it overlooked the extent to which parliamentary institutions have lost their stature as free expressions of popular sovereignty. No one who observes government after government formed by electoral pluralities or who watches the management of Parliament by political party mandarins could possibly confuse these institutional anomalies with "rule by the people." But whatever their imperfections, parliamentary institutions are more appropriate political forums for legitimizing some notion of the people's will than are courts.

But whether the courts or legislatures assume the task, there is still no absolute way of protecting rights, no matter how diligently we may try to tack down the language of any charter. Nor is there any charter which will not give rise to the need for political judgements, the balancing of collective demands and individual rights. In this exercise, there are no guarantees that either courts or legislatures will be seats of unblemished reason; indeed the evidence suggests that frequently they will both fall short of expectations. In that sense, the continuing struggle to preserve human rights ultimately devolves upon the people themselves. If that is the case, the existing balance of judicial and legislative powers over protections of rights in the Canadian Charter of Human Rights and Freedoms is entirely appropriate.

Canadian courts now have the clear mandate and authority to protect human rights by striking down any provincial or federal laws which in their opinion violate the charter. Moreover, they may do so without great anguishing over the effects their decisions might have on public policy, since the notwithstanding clause gives citizens a final recourse to legislatures over many of these matters. There is therefore little reason why judges should not be as "activist" as their own philosophies will permit them. Legislatures for their part have the right to act to enlarge freedoms in advance of the judicial system and ultimately to overrule the courts in certain areas whenever they think the public interest requires it. Both systems can therefore benefit Canadians even if neither system is foolproof. Under these circumstances, the Canadian Charter of Rights and Freedoms ought to improve the prospects for a more humane country.

### The Charter's Role in the New Federalism: Symbols and Practice

But the nation-building potential of the charter may prove to be the more profound, if the least recognized, of its purposes. Although the principal target of such nation building was always Quebec separatism and the wider resolution of French-English relations, the national importance of the charter will go beyond matters of linguistic justice. In the course of the political battle, it became evident that the charter had broad support throughout the country. Over time, it should become an even more venerable symbol of Canadians' collective political identity. If the Supreme Court carries out the national mandate to declare and unify our values on the basis of this charter, its national significance as both symbol and foundation for this country can hardly be overstated.

Canadian political culture has never rested on foundation documents of this kind, but the pivotal role of such constitutional documents can be seen in the political culture of other societies, especially that of our close neighbour the United States. If the the Canadian charter serves anything like the purpose of its American counterpart, it will help institutionalize a national creed and pattern of political values quite different from those that Premier Sterling Lyon unsuccessfully tried to defend in the First Ministers' Conference in September 1980. In fact the massive public support for the charter already suggested at that time that the vitality of the older tradition of parliamentary sovereignty was in doubt. Although, as part of the intergovernmental bargain, the notwithstanding clause concedes the option of a parliamentary override of certain rights in the charter, the weight of public opinion is already stacked against any government which would invoke the theory of "parliamentary sovereignty" against the "people's" rights and freedoms. This development has to be regarded as dramatic in a polity built upon parliamentary institutions.

It was not long after the new constitution became law, however, before the first use was made of the notwithstanding clause. As part of its rearguard campaign against the new constitution, the PQ government introduced Bill 62 on May 5, 1982. It sought to exempt Quebecers completely from fundamental, legal and equality rights under the constitution, and to reaffirm the principle of limiting access to English schools for anglophones from other provinces. Although the PQ government had an appealing justification for its action — that it wished to exempt Quebec as much as possible from the constitution to which it had not consented — its political position may not in the long run be easy to maintain. Legislating against basic freedoms has to be a politically dubious course of action; and even if the political climate may permit such a law in 1982, circumstances may not be as propitious in 1987 or 1992 when the restrictions will have to be renewed. But since individual rights in Quebec are subordinated to the collective issues of language and francophone survival, the final outcome cannot be foreseen.

Still, since the charter will declare overwhelmingly

*national* values which cannot be appropriated by the spokesmen of regionalism, the nation-building value of the charter as ideology is clear. It is the role of the Supreme Court as a national institution expounding and applying the charter which ought in practice to tip the balance of power in Canadian federalism toward the centre. Once again, American experience suggests that a court bound to apply a common set of political values as enshrined in a constitutional bill of rights must set aside regional particularisms whenever they conflict. Provincial laws which in one way or another discriminate between citizens by reasons of residence in violation of the principles of the new charter shall be declared null and void by the courts. Under such circumstances, Ottawa would acquire a powerful new ally in any campaign against regionalism.

## The Charter's Role in the New Federalism: Language Rights

The linguistic provisions of the Canada Act deserve careful scrutiny, first in terms of their own strengths and weaknesses in the light of the Liberal strategy to win over francophone Quebecers to homeland Canada, and secondly from a broader historical and political perspective. The language provisions of the Canada Act were soon denounced in Quebec for threatening the linguistic security of francophones *and* anglophones; reactions outside Quebec, especially in Western Canada, were often no more temperate. While some denounced the constitution's unrealistic extension of bilingualism, Canada's commissioner of official languages in his 1981 annual report derided the new constitution for not going far enough.

However they look from partisan standpoints, the

new provisions from section 16 through 23 constitute something of a revolution in terms of the previous constitutional status of French-English relations. The constitutional entrenchment of bilingualism is a significant step beyond the statutory provisions of the 1968 Official Languages Act and a giant step beyond the constitutional status quo. In fourteen years the recognition of the French fact has been extended from its acknowledged status in Quebec and the federal Parliament under the BNA Act to a position of constitutional equality with English all across Canada. In addition, New Brunswick has become officially bilingual, while Manitoba was restored to that condition by a court order in 1979. In 1982 only Ontario remained outside the bloc of new bilingual provinces which is intended to make Quebecers feel more at home in the country.

Similarly, when compared to the past, the record on minority language educational rights has to be acknowledged as significantly changed. For the first time in Canadian history, publicly funded, French language educational rights have been enshrined for the official linguistic minorities everywhere "where numbers warrant." English-language educational rights have been entrenched for the children of most English-speaking Canadians who either live in Quebec or might move to the province. Although such rights had been accepted in principle by provincial governments in 1977, it has now become constitutionally binding on all provinces without any recourse to a legislative override.

The weaknesses in these provisions, however, are not hard to identify. One of the most glaring is the exclusion of Ontario from the bilingual bloc. Both by geography and by number of francophones, Ontario was a logical province to accept bilingual status, but the Conservative Davis government resisted on financial and political grounds. Yet Ontario's failure only strengthens the resolve of the francophone majority in Quebec not to be unduly generous with its anglophone minority. And although Quebec anglophones have always enjoyed a much stronger position than have their francophone counterparts elsewhere, as a result of the Canada Act the fates of the linguistic minorities have never been more obviously linked. For example, mirroring the disappointment of Ontario francophones with the constitution is the dismay of Quebec anglophones over Ottawa's excluding them from the protection of one of the education provisions. Under section 59, unless the Quebec government or legislature later agrees to extend such protection, minority language educational rights can be restricted to the children of those who themselves attended English schools in Canada or who had or have children studying in English in Canada. This exception effectively cuts off any strength the educational system of the minority might have drawn from immigration. In the light of a weakened anglophone presence in Quebec and of the conclusions of scholars such as Richard Joy who reported in 1978 that the French language and culture were "completely secure within the province of Quebec," this retreat by the federal Liberals must seem neither just nor necessary.

Criticisms have also been raised over other deficiencies, such as the omission of bilingual government services from most provinces and the ineffectiveness of bilingual guarantees in the court system. The qualification "where numbers warrant" on minority language educational rights has also been attacked for offering too niggling a restriction. Yet some practical limit upon this right would have had to be imposed. In that sense, the words acknowledge that such rights are not boundless or absolute, and they leave the question of settling on what are "warrantable numbers" to the discretion of the courts. More critical perhaps to linguistic minorities is the failure to grant explicit minority control of minority language educational facilities in the constitution. Effective educational protection may depend upon linguistic minorities having their own school boards. While a liberal court interpretation of "educational facilities" under section 23(3)(b) could provide minorities with that control, the vagueness of the section is not encouraging. The same ambiguity arises over whether mixed or bilingual schools would satisfy the constitutional requirement for educational facilities. If they do, minority groups are likely to be less than satisfied with the arrangement. Since only Supreme Court interpretations of the language guarantees will answer these questions, the value of the linguistic bargain will depend on the political strategy of leaving such questions to the judiciary, without recourse to a legislative override.

All these criticisms suggest that conflict between the two founding language groups will persist in Canada. But the fact that the constitution will not immediately usher in a period of linguistic peace and justice is no reason to ignore the achievements that have been won. Even with all the practical drawbacks, the language guarantees symbolize a new French-English partnership.

It may seem odd to refer to such a partnership while the government of Quebec refuses to consent to it. But Quebec supported the essentials of such a partnership when, in 1977, Premier Lévesque signed an interprovincial memorandum of understanding promising Quebec's "best efforts to provide instruction in education in English and French wherever numbers warrant." That principle, unanimously adopted by the premiers, is now enshrined in the constitution so that it cannot later be disregarded or repudiated.

What will challenge the new linguistic bargain more than politics, however, will be whether bilingualism is practical. Critics have argued that it cannot withstand the homogenizing pressures of modern life. To them the language provisions in the new constitution are artificial measures which cannot protect minorities from gradual assimilation and thus prevent the ultimate development of two Canadas — one totally French-speaking, the other English. With the numbers of the linguistic minorities dropping in predominantly English- and French-speaking parts of Canada, the critics contend that Trudeau's bilingual option is doomed.

It is too soon to write obituaries for bilingualism. Although the strength of the francophone minorities outside the so-called bilingual belt of northern New Brunswick and northeastern Ontario is eroding seriously, new economic and demographic factors could alter that picture as rapidly as they have in the past. Since the economic base for the francophone homeland in Quebec is weakening and the economic growth in other areas, especially in Western Canada, is only now beginning to show its potential, circumstances may cause a larger francophone migration, and a greater need for a bilingual infrastructure. The requirement of bilingualism for Canada's future elite will also have its effect; it has already resulted in successful French immersion classes in predominantly anglophone parts of Canada. Immigration to Canada may also have an important long-term effect, as those born with English as their native tongue are displaced. These and other variables may make the politics of bilingualism attractive for more than symbolic reasons. But in an overwhelming English-speaking North America, it must be admitted the odds are not promising.

## Aboriginal Rights

What the new constitutional agreement may mean for aboriginal peoples was extremely unclear as the Canada Act was passed. The legal and political dimensions of the problem are complex; they call for remarkably sensitive treatment by the Supreme Court of Canada. In fact, so open-ended are the questions that the fate of native rights will depend at least as much on the philosophy and direction the court adopts towards the entire Charter of Rights as upon the language of the charter or the history of native law. In that respect, the general cautions concerning judicial statecraft raised earlier are pertinent.

On balance, the new native rights provisions probably will improve the relative position of aboriginal peoples. One can hazard this opinion partly because native rights enjoyed so perilous a status in Canadian law that they can hardly decline, and partly because of some promising possibilities in new sections of the constitution.

On the defensive front, section 25 protects native peoples from any possible reduction in their unique treaty or other rights arising from all citizens' standard rights, especially from demands for equality under section 15. In addition, the provision for affirmative action programs in section 15(2) allows and, as suggested earlier, may even encourage governmental initiatives to advance aboriginal rights. Section 37, by setting aboriginal rights on the agenda of the next constitutional conference and by providing for native representation, gives to aboriginal rights a new political visibility. Such an opportunity to advance a case for fundamental justice for native peoples under the Canadian Charter of Rights could make a significant difference to how native issues are legislated, even if it is unlikely to deflect the drive towards resource development in the North and elsewhere.

The most problematic element in the package on native rights, however, is section 35 in which "the existing aboriginal and treaty rights of the aboriginal peoples of Canada are hereby recognized and affirmed." This was the section which was struck out of the constitutional agreement during the negotiations of November 1981 and was restored (with the word "existing" added) by public lobbying. It raises the most ambiguity about the future rights of native peoples. It can be read in two distinct ways: the first is that section 35 offers constitutional recognition of the admittedly weak position of aboriginal treaty rights in the statute and common law as of the date of proclamation; the second is that aboriginal and treaty rights themselves are accorded constitutional protection in the sense that no statute may infringe them.

It was certainly the view of the federal government that only the first meaning applied. So concerned were they that native rights, especially land claims, not stand in the way of economic development that Justice Minister Chrétien refused to write in the principle of native consent prior to any extinguishing of aboriginal land rights. If the first view is correct, there is little additional protection for native peoples from this section; at best it is a mere declaration of good intent, at worst simply a public relations exercise.

If the second reading of section 35 is accepted, the courts may be forced to depart from earlier legislative history and place native treaty rights on at least as strong a plane as other rights. Hence, since the not-withstanding clause is not applicable, these rights may be put beyond the ordinary reach of legislative enactment. Whether this direction is adopted will depend largely on what position the court adopts toward the rights in the charter as a whole. At least until "aboriginal rights" are more precisely defined by constitutional amendment, possibly following the next constitutional conference, the courts will have wide latitude in interpreting and giving effect to such rights.

What may strengthen the second interpretation on behalf of native rights is section 52. The first part of this section leaves no doubt that any law inconsistent with the constitution of Canada shall have "no force," and the second part declares the constitution of Canada to include, among other matters, the order admitting Rupert's Land and the North-Western Territory to Canada. Since that order contained provisions acknowledging aboriginal rights and requiring equity in any extinguishment of these rights, these may now be "entrenched" rights in the sense that they cannot be overturned by any act of Parliament. When this section is read together with section 35, it would appear that there is a stronger case for resolving any ambiguity in section 35 in favour of native rights.

But the political repercussions from the two readings of section 35 are stark and dramatic. The first reading leaves Parliament ultimately with a free hand to deal with native peoples' rights in whatever way it wishes. The second places a constitutional barrier to Parliamentary management of native land claims — surrender of these rights could only be accomplished by constitutional amendment. Since the latter option is likely to be regarded by the courts as unworkable, the politics of the second interpretation of section 35 does not appear encouraging for native peoples. In addition, since the politics is likely to be most sensitive on land rights issues, it may well be that courts will compensate by being more generous in recognizing cultural rights of native peoples. Only the evolving philosophy and politics of the judiciary will provide final answers to such complex legal and political issues.

## Equalization and Resource Powers

Although part III, titled "Equalization and Regional Disparities," is widely separated in the resolution from part VI, which deals with natural resources, in a sense they represent an entente between the wealthier producing provinces, only recently emerging from the have-not camp, and the other have-not provinces. There was no dispute over the principle of equalization. That it could be declared and enshrined in the constitution after a quarter century is a testament to the vision of John Diefenbaker, who in 1957 first instituted equalization payments. Since the section dealing with equalization is merely a general statement of principle, however, it is doubtful whether it would be an effective defence for any have-not provinces fighting federal cutbacks. On resource questions, a remarkable acquiescence to increased provincial powers has emerged, even though the wealth and importance of resources varies tremendously between provinces. Overcoming these differences was a noteworthy achievement in no small measure due to the dramatic rise of Western Canadian leadership.

The idea for the new powers set out in part VI goes back to the constitutional conferences of Western premiers held from 1976 on. Premier Blakeney, having suffered two major setbacks in the courts over his potash rationing scheme and oil and gas royalties tax, convinced his colleagues to press for strengthened provincial powers. Specifically, Saskatchewan wanted powers over interprovincial and international trade in natural resources, as well as the power of indirect taxation of natural resources. These proposals, if taken at face value, would permit the resource-rich provinces to set their own prices for natural resources, short of a federal declaration of an emergency. The Western provinces also wanted the federal government to cede its declaratory power (section 92, 10 (c)) over natural resources which would otherwise legally have permitted Ottawa to take over works under provincial control and ownership whenever it declared them "to be for the general advantage of Canada." Against a background of escalating tensions between Ottawa and the West during the energy crisis, the Western provinces came to see these matters as their top constitutional priority.

The new constitution reflects federal willingness to accommodate these demands within limits. The provinces are given much more explicitly defined powers over non-renewable natural resources, forestry resources and electrical energy. Some of the critical areas conceded exclusively to the provinces include exploration, development and management of resources, including rates of primary production. These are all matters in which it might also be said a national interest is and has been at stake, especially in the National Energy Program's goal of self-sufficiency. These exclusive powers can easily set off a new series of court challenges over federal initiatives in the resource development and exploration field, the outcome of which may leave the federal Parliament with much more reduced powers.

The limits imposed on provincial powers over interprovincial trade in these natural resources bar "discrimination in prices or in supplies exported to another part of Canada." Although this qualification prevents blatant interprovincial preferences, it opens the door for more attempts by the resource-rich provinces to control the national market in key resources. Even if Parliament has the ability to override the provinces in this respect under subsection (3), the federal power may come to be exercised only in exceptional circumstances and end up in substance, if not in form, as an emergency power. The same danger arises in the provincial field of indirect taxation on resources. Although outright discrimination is prevented, the scope of provincial regulation over the national market in key areas of the economy has been significantly enlarged and the moral case for asserting a national presence has been weakened except in compelling circumstances. These two new provincial powers may come to be recognized as a significant devolution of power, far more problematical in effect than its framers anticipated.

## Canada's New Amending Formula

In Chapter 1 an amending formula was said to describe a pattern of power relationships of enduring importance to a nation. That explains in part why an agreement was so difficult to obtain. But now that we have a formula, it should be possible to examine these new relationships between provinces, regions and the national Parliament.

First of all, it is obvious that Alberta, as the principal architect of the new formula, has won. Moreover it has won with a formula which, as late as the summer of 1980, many governments had not taken seriously. That remarkable achievement was made possible because the federal unilateral policy threw Quebec into the arms of the Western-dominated Gang of Eight. To forge its ties of solidarity against Trudeau, the gang coalesced around the only "provincial" amending formula still in the running against the Victoria Charter. On April 16, 1981, the Constitutional Accord was signed declaring the modified Alberta formula as the gang's common position. To sign, Quebec ceded its veto over constitutional amendments in return for a purely defensive power of opting out and receiving compensation. At the time, Quebec no doubt considered its consent to be a temporary tactical ploy to preserve an alliance against federal heavy-handedness, but it had, as described earlier, unforeseen consequences.

Eventually Ontario joined Quebec in ceding its right to a veto; thus no province stood opposed to the principle of equality among the provinces in the amending formula. By breaking away from its traditional Central Canadian alliance with Ontario, Quebec had abandoned the claims of both provinces for pre-eminence. The permanent grip of Ontario and Quebec on all constitutional changes was therefore loosened and the power of each dramatically reduced. Constitutional change, except for those limited matters requiring unanimity outlined in section 41, could now proceed with agreement by the House of Commons and seven provinces representing at least 50 per cent of the population of all the provinces. That would currently require the consent of Ontario *or* Quebec.

When it is recognized that the regional definitions in the Victoria formula merely repeat the logic of existing provincial inequalities in representation in the Senate, the revolutionary nature of the new principle of provincial equality becomes evident. It overturns assumptions built into the Canadian constitution and makes equality of representation by provinces in a reformed Senate a real possibility. This "roll-over effect" of the equality principle is likely, despite the fact that the two issues are not at all the same. Since at least seven provinces have already affirmed the principle of provincial equality in a new Senate, and since changes in Senate composition do not require unanimity, the long-term prospects are excellent for carrying forward provincial equality under the amending formula to reform of the Senate. Such a change would reshape the Canadian federation, remove at least in a formal sense the dominance of Central Canada, and align Canadian federalism more closely with most other federal states in fundamental principles (i.e., state equality).

Therefore the new amending formula made a much more dramatic case for genuine constitutional renewal than did the Victoria formula. It helped overcome regional rancour, but more importantly it brought constitutional formalism closer to actual Canadian conditions. An economic and political realignment of power away from Central Canada is already in process; it would therefore have been absurd to graft on outmoded assumptions from Canada's first century of experience.

But the amendment procedure not only scraps the legal notion of Central Canadian dominance, it also signifies the virtual extinction of the compact theory of Confederation. Whatever the court pronouncements on the principle of duality with respect to the passing of the Canada Act, and whatever might be said about Confederation as a bargain between the English- and French-speaking peoples, there is no room for its recognition in the new amending formula. While other provisions in the package set out a new French-English partnership in the country which dramatically improves on the state of affairs under the old 1867 constitution, Quebec's special character as the only francophone province in Canada has not been acknowledged. And while the right to "opt out" and thus protect its own jurisdiction is still secure, Quebec's broader historic mandate as the spokesman and guarantor of the French people in Canada has suffered a setback. Broad responsibility for the protection of the French language and peoples in Canada has now been legally assumed by the courts. This reduction in Quebec's national role as would-be protector of the French language in Canada has been the direct political consequence of most Quebecers' withdrawal to, and preoccupation with, the Quebec state.

Although Trudeau went on record as deeply regretting the scrapping of the idea of constitutional change by referenda, it would probably be more accurate to say that he really lamented the ceding of federal control by means of referenda rather than referenda as such. At no time in all the debates did Trudeau budge from unilateral federal control of this option. It is therefore reasonable to conclude that it was more federal power than democratic principle which motivated the central government. Properly conceived and with equality of access by either level of government, the referendum proposal might have proved a worthwhile alternative to intergovernmental dead-lock, but it was a power play from the start. Given the efforts at governmental manipulation of public opinion through mass advertising techniques on the constitutional front, among others, it is probably just as well that the idea was put to rest.

The remarkable feature of the general amending formula is surely the provision for "opting out." Up to three provinces may dissent from amendments affecting their powers as set out in section 38 (3). No amendment binds every government, no matter how high the level of popular support for it. But this feature, if unusual, is not unprecedented since it was considered for restricted use in 1936. The idea rests on two principles: first, that no province ought to have its constitutional rights and powers reduced without its consent; second, that no single province ought to block others from making desired changes whenever there is a general will to do so. Earlier amendment formulae had tried to answer the first concern with a unanimity rule which negated the second. Others like the Victoria formula conceded the first principle to Ontario and Quebec and left other provinces unprotected. Still other formulae had tried to sort out the dilemma by arbitrarily declaring vital and less vital areas of provincial powers, with the latter category only protected by the rule of consent. Of all the proposals advanced so far, the present arrangement best preserves the balance between each province's consent and flexibility for constitutional change.

The drawback to this idea is said to be the "checker-board effect." Opting out could lead to a "checker-board" Canada if several amendments passed with only partial consent by the provinces. A citizen could then find that a constitutional regime applied in one province but not in another—indeed that a constitutional roadmap might be required to find out which provinces are "in" or "out" on any given constitutional subject. But the Parliament of Canada retains the right to decide at every point what political gain or cost is to be achieved from each amendment and may refuse its assent to amendments on which it would prefer more agreement. It holds the power to prevent checkerboarding, as do any like-minded group of four premiers.

A number of commentators, including veteran secretary to Liberal cabinets Gordon Robertson, have argued that the opting-out provisions may lead to constitutional inflexibility. Their argument is that Parliament may not pass amendments unless they carry unanimous provincial consent. Such a position assumes that the alleged nuisance of opting out will be so deleterious that future Parliaments will prefer immovability over desired constitutional change. Whether Parliaments will take this categorical stand remains to be seen, but the threat of opting out may well limit the pace of constitutional change. In the last analysis, it will be up to the judgement of each federal government to weigh in each circumstance the benefits from any amendment against the cost of opting out.

The other methods of amendment of the constitution where changes affect one level only (sections 44 and 45) or some provinces but not all (section 43) simply continue existing practice. All provinces will be reassured however by the explicit provision that boundaries between provinces may not be altered without the consent of Ottawa and the affected provinces. Another welcome addition from the unilateral package as finalized by Parliament was the inclusion of an override on the Senate over constitutional amendments. With Senate reform itself a subject for constitutional talks, it would have been unthinkable to leave the veto with the Senate.

## Conclusion

Even though the new Canadian constitution does not repeal the substance of the old constitution but mostly renames certain earlier enactments and adds the various sections described in Appendix 1, it has permanently altered the nature of the Canadian federal state. Though clearly the product of compromise, the new constitution is on balance a better piece of constitutional handiwork than the unilateral federal document or any of the earlier draft versions. The Charter of Rights is stronger and more comprehensive than before, its provisions as toughly worded as the process of lobbying on Parliament during the winter of 1980-81 could make them. New rights for the disadvantaged — native peoples, the handicapped, women — were written in. At the same time, the dangers of ultimate judicial law-making were precluded, with the political onus for overriding the judiciary's interpretation on certain individual rights placed squarely where it belongs — on the shoulders of politically accountable legislatures. Futhermore, the informal effects of the notwithstanding clause are likely to make both agencies — courts and legislatures — more vigilant and aware of human rights than in the past.

Moreover the amending formula declared a new federal order in Canada where even the weakest and smallest province, Prince Edward Island, can look for a fairer set of relationships. The preponderances of wealth and population were challenged in this round of talks and, since the formula is more flexible than most expected, the possibility for carrying through the principle of equality among provinces in subsequent negotiations is strong. If that principle is accorded its due status in a reconstituted second federal chamber such as the "Council of the Provinces," Canadians will have a chance to see how important the amending formula victory really was.

The new constitution also attempted to restructure Canadian federalism in the light of separatism in Quebec and regionalism elsewhere. The French-English conflict was addressed in terms of guaranteed official linguistic equality and access to schooling in either official tongue, while the political burden of defending these rights was shifted to the courts. Although Quebec is as well armed as all other provinces in defending its own jurisdiction by the right to "opt out," the defence of linguistic minorities elsewhere has been assumed by the judiciary. This reversed Quebec's moral role as guarantor, just as it undermined the legal protectorship of Parliament under the old constitution. Confederation had originally granted power to Parliament to protect the rights of denominational (and thus indirectly linguistic) minorities in the provinces. Under section 93 Parliament could pass remedial legislation to overcome any prejudicial actions taken by provinces. The history of abuses especially to French-speaking minorities in many provinces is eloquent testimony to the failure of that theory of Parliamentary guardianship. By entrenching these rights, Parliament has tacitly admitted that this role as defender of linguistic minorities in the provinces should be assumed by an independent judiciary.

As with language rights, so too with human rights. In large part these were entrusted to the care of the courts who will help check governmental abuses of the individual rights of citizens. Both roles for the courts present new and difficult challenges to Canadian federalism. But the strength of the strategy finally depends on Canadians' commitment to the Charter of Rights as a new compact between English- and French-speaking federalists, as well as a compact over the rights of individual citizens and the powers of governments. In either sense, the constitution will be a document of extraordinary national significance.

Of course, the work of constitutional renewal did not end with patriation. There remain many pressing changes that must be made if the continuing crises afflicting Confederation are to be addressed and turned back. Certainly there will be recurring discontent if this constitutional agenda is thought to *complete* the process. Quebecers who voted for the federalist option in the referendum will probably want more change. Many other provinces whose agendas were put on the back burner will want them addressed. But the new constitution will permit Canadians to make these changes more quickly and easily.

The acid test of the new constitution will come, however, only when the English- and French-speaking peoples of Canada try to come to terms with their new partnership. For those who see self-determination for Quebec as the only guarantee of survival for the Québécois, there can of course be no peace with this constitutional settlement. For those who have always thought of Canada as basically anglophone with adjustments for francophones largely in or adjacent to Quebec, the settlement will seem an impertinent extension of French power. Certainly the constitutional entrenchment of bilingual rights does radically redefine the nature of the Canadian state; historians may therefore have to join with the late Donald Creighton in labelling Trudeau's enterprise as a constitutional revolution. But even for those who are inclined to think about Canada in these terms, the bilingual vision may not in the long run seem either practical or adequate. Perhaps it is little more than a bold gamble dependent for its success on good luck and on a severe test of Canadians' national will. In that sense, the success of the idea will depend on whether the Canadian people can or want to live up to the legal architecture. The answer to that question awaits us in time.

# Appendix 1
# Canada Act

An Act to give effect to a request by the Senate and House of Commons of Canada

Whereas Canada has requested and consented to the enactment of an Act of the Parliament of the United Kingdom to give effect to the provisions hereinafter set forth and the Senate and the House of Commons of Canada in Parliament assembled have submitted an address to Her Majesty requesting that Her Majesty may graciously be pleased to cause a Bill to be laid before the Parliament of the United Kingdom for that purpose.

Be it therefore enacted by the Queen's Most Excellent Majesty, by and with the advice and consent of the Lords Spiritual and Temporal, and Commons, in this present Parliament assembled, and by the authority of the same, as follows:

*Constitution Act, 1981 enacted*

**1.** The *Constitution Act, 1981* set out in Schedule B to this Act is hereby enacted for and shall have the force of law in Canada and shall come into force as provided in that Act.

*Termination of power to legislate for Canada*

**2.** No Act of the Parliament of the United Kingdom passed after the *Constitution Act, 1981* comes into force shall extend to Canada as part of its law.

French version  **3.** So far as it is not contained in Schedule B, the French version of this Act is set out in Schedule A to this Act and has the same authority in Canada as the English version thereof.

Short title  **4.** This Act may be cited as the *Canada Act*.

# CONSTITUTION ACT, 1981

**PART I**             **SCHEDULE B**

# CANADIAN CHARTER OF RIGHTS AND FREEDOMS

Whereas Canada is founded upon principles that recognize the supremacy of God and the rule of law:

### *Guarantee of Rights and Freedoms*

Rights and freedoms in Canada  **1.** The *Canadian Charter of Rights and Freedoms* guarantees the rights and freedoms set out in it subject only to such reasonable limits prescribed by law as can be demonstrably justified in a free and democratic society.

### *Fundamental Freedoms*

Fundamental freedoms  **2.** Everyone has the following fundamental freedoms:
    (*a*) freedom of conscience and religion;
    (*b*) freedom of thought, belief, opinion and expression, including freedom of the press and other media of communication;
    (*c*) freedom of peaceful assembly; and
    (*d*) freedom of association.

## Democratic Rights

Democratic
rights of
citizens

**3.** Every citizen of Canada has the right to vote in an election of members of the House of Commons or of a legislative assembly and to be qualified for membership therein.

Maximum
duration of
legislative
bodies

**4.** (1) No House of Commons and no legislative assembly shall continue for longer than five years from the date fixed for the return of the writs at a general election of its members.

Continuation in
special
circumstances

(2) In time of real or apprehended war, invasion or insurrection, a House of Commons may be continued by Parliament and a legislative assembly may be continued by the legislature beyond five years if such continuation is not opposed by the votes of more than one-third of the members of the House of Commons or the legislative assembly, as the case may be.

Annual sitting
of legislative
bodies

**5.** There shall be a sitting of Parliament and of each legislature at least once every twelve months.

## Mobility Rights

Mobility of
citizens

**6.** (1) Every citizen of Canada has the right to enter, remain in and leave Canada.

Rights to move
and gain
livelihood

(2) Every citizen of Canada and every person who has the status of a permanent resident of Canada has the right
    (*a*) to move to and take up residence in any province; and
    (*b*) to pursue the gaining of a livelihood in any province.

Limitation

(3) The rights specified in subsection (2) are subject to
    (*a*) any laws or practices of general application in force in a province other than those that discriminate among persons primarily on the basis of province of present or previous residence; and

(b) any laws providing for reasonable residency requirements as a qualification for the receipt of publicly provided social services.

Affirmative action programs

(4) Subsections (2) and (3) do not preclude any law, program or activity that has as its object the amelioration in a province of conditions of individuals in that province who are socially or economically disadvantaged if the rate of employment in that province is below the rate of employment in Canada.

### Legal Rights

Life, liberty and security of person

7. Everyone has the right to life, liberty and security of the person and the right not to be deprived thereof except in accordance with the principles of fundamental justice.

Search or seizure

8. Everyone has the right to be secure against unreasonable search or seizure.

Detention or imprisonment

9. Everyone has the right not to be arbitrarily detained or imprisoned.

Arrest or detention

10. Everyone has the right on arrest or detention
(a) to be informed promptly of the reasons therefor;
(b) to retain and instruct counsel without delay and to be informed of that right; and
(c) to have the validity of the detention determined by way of *habeas corpus* and to be released if the detention is not lawful.

Proceedings in criminal and penal matters

11. Any person charged with an offence has the right
(a) to be informed without unreasonable delay of the specific offence;
(b) to be tried within a reasonable time;
(c) not to be compelled to be a witness in proceedings against that person in respect of the offence;
(d) to be presumed innocent until proven guilty according to law in a fair and public hearing by an independent and impartial tribunal;
(e) not to be denied reasonable bail without just cause;

(*f*) except in the case of an offence under military law tried before a military tribunal, to the benefit of trial by jury where the maximum punishment for the offence is imprisonment for five years or a more severe punishment;

(*g*) not to be found guilty on account of any act or omission unless, at the time of the act or omission, it constituted an offence under Canadian or international law or was criminal according to the general principles of law recognized by the community of nations;

(*h*) if finally acquitted of the offence, not to be tried for it again and, if finally found guilty and punished for the offence, not to be tried or punished for it again; and

(*i*) if found guilty of the offence and if the punishment for the offence has been varied between the time of commission and the time of sentencing, to the benefit of the lesser punishment.

**Treatment or punishment**

**12.** Everyone has the right not to be subjected to any cruel and unusual treatment or punishment.

**Self-crimination**

**13.** A witness who testifies in any proceedings has the right not to have any incriminating evidence so given used to incriminate that witness in any other proceedings, except in a prosecution for perjury or for the giving of contradictory evidence.

**Interpreter**

**14.** A party or witness in any proceedings who does not understand or speak the language in which the proceedings are conducted or who is deaf has the right to the assistance of an interpreter.

## *Equality Rights*

**Equality before and under law and equal protection and benefit of law**

**15.** (1) Every individual is equal before and under the law and has the right to the equal protection and equal benefit of the law without discrimination and, in particular, without discrimination based on race, national or ethnic origin, colour, religion, sex, age or mental or physical disability.

**Affirmative action programs**

(2) Subsection (1) does not preclude any law, program or activity that has as its object the amelioration of

conditions of disadvantaged individuals or groups including those that are disadvantaged because of race, national or ethnic origin, colour, religion, sex, age or mental or physical disability.

## Official Languages of Canada

Official languages of Canada

**16.** (1) English and French are the official languages of Canada and have equality of status and equal rights and privileges as to their use in all institutions of the Parliament and government of Canada.

Official languages of New Brunswick

(2) English and French are the official languages of New Brunswick and have equality of status and equal rights and privileges as to their use in all institutions of the legislature and government of New Brunswick.

Advancement of status and use

(3) Nothing in this Charter limits the authority of Parliament or a legislature to advance the equality of status or use of English and French.

Proceedings of Parliament

**17.** (1) Everyone has the right to use English or French in any debates and other proceedings of Parliament.

Proceedings of New Brunswick legislature

(2) Everyone has the right to use English or French in any debates and other proceedings of the legislature of New Brunswick.

Parliamentary statutes and records

**18.** (1) The statutes, records and journals of Parliament shall be printed and published in English and French and both language versions are equally authoritative.

New Brunswick statutes and records

(2) The statutes, records and journals of the legislature of New Brunswick shall be printed and published in English and French and both language versions are equally authoritative.

Proceedings in courts established by Parliament

**19.** (1) Either English or French may be used by any person in, or in any pleading in or process issuing from, any court established by Parliament.

Proceedings in
New Brunswick
courts

(2) Either English or French may be used by any person in, or in any pleading in or process issuing from, any court of New Brunswick.

Communications by public
with federal
institutions

**20.** (1) Any member of the public in Canada has the right to communicate with, and to receive available services from, any head or central office of an institution of the Parliament or government of Canada in English or French, and has the same right with respect to any other office of any such institution where

(*a*) there is a significant demand for communications with and services from that office in such language; or

(*b*) due to the nature of the office, it is reasonable that communications with and services from that office be available in both English and French.

Communications by public
with New
Brunswick
institutions

(2) Any member of the public in New Brunswick has the right to communicate with, and to receive available services from, any office of an institution of the legislature or government of New Brunswick in English or French.

Continuation of
existing
constitutional
provisions

**21.** Nothing in sections 16 to 20 abrogates or derogates from any right, privilege or obligation with respect to the English and French languages, or either of them, that exists or is continued by virtue of any other provision of the Constitution of Canada.

Rights and
privileges
preserved

**22.** Nothing in sections 16 to 20 abrogates or derogates from any legal or customary right or privilege acquired or enjoyed either before or after the coming into force of this Charter with respect to any language that is not English or French.

### *Minority Language Educational Rights*

Language of
instruction

**23.** (1) Citizens of Canada

(*a*) whose first language learned and still understood is that of the English or French linguistic minority population of the province in which they reside, or

(*b*) who have received their primary school instruction in Canada in English or French and reside in a province where the language in which they received that instruction is the language of the English or French linguistic minority population of the province,

have the right to have their children receive primary and secondary school instruction in that language in that province.

**Continuity of language instruction**

(2) Citizens of Canada of whom any child has received or is receiving primary or secondary school instruction in English or French in Canada, have the right to have all their children receive primary and secondary school instruction in the same language.

**Application where numbers warrant**

(3) The right of citizens of Canada under subsections (1) and (2) to have their children receive primary and secondary school instruction in the language of the English or French linguistic minority population of a province

(a) applies wherever in the province the number of children of citizens who have such a right is sufficient to warrant the provision to them out of public funds of minority language instruction; and

(b) includes, where the number of those children so warrants, the right to have them receive that instruction in minority language educational facilities provided out of public funds.

## Enforcement

**Enforcement of guaranteed rights and freedoms**

**24.** (1) Anyone whose rights or freedoms, as guaranteed by this Charter, have been infringed or denied may apply to a court of competent jurisdiction to obtain such remedy as the court considers appropriate and just in the circumstances.

**Exclusion of evidence bringing administration of justice into disrepute**

(2) Where, in proceedings under subsection (1), a court concludes that evidence was obtained in a manner that infringed or denied any rights or freedoms guaranteed by this Charter, the evidence shall be excluded if it is established that, having regard to all the circumstances, the admission of it in the proceedings would bring the administration of justice into disrepute.

## General

**Aboriginal rights and freedoms not affected by Charter**

**25.** The guarantee in this Charter of certain rights and freedoms shall not be construed so as to abrogate or derogate from any aboriginal, treaty or other rights or freedoms that pertain to the aboriginal peoples of Canada including

(*a*) any rights or freedoms that have been recognized by the Royal Proclamation of October 7, 1763; and

(*b*) any rights or freedoms that may be acquired by the aboriginal peoples of Canada by way of land claims settlement.

**Other rights and freedoms not affected by Charter**

**26.** The guarantee in this Charter of certain rights and freedoms shall not be construed as denying the existence of any other rights or freedoms that exist in Canada.

**Multicultural heritage**

**27.** This Charter shall be interpreted in a manner consistent with the preservation and enhancement of the multicultural heritage of Canadians.

**Rights guaranteed equally to both sexes**

**28.** Notwithstanding anything in this Charter, the rights and freedoms referred to in it are guaranteed equally to male and female persons.

**Rights respecting certain schools preserved**

**29.** Nothing in this Charter abrogates or derogates from any rights or privileges guaranteed by or under the Constitution of Canada in respect of denominational, separate or dissentient schools.

**Application to territories and territorial authorities**

**30.** A reference in this Charter to a province or to the legislative assembly or legislature of a province shall be deemed to include a reference to the Yukon Territory and the Northwest Territories, or to the appropriate legislative authority thereof, as the case may be.

**Legislative powers not extended**

**31.** Nothing in this Charter extends the legislative powers of any body or authority.

## Application of Charter

**Application of Charter**

**32.** (1) This Charter applies

(*a*) to the Parliament and government of Canada in respect of all matters within the authority of Parliament including all matters relating to the Yukon Territory and Northwest Territories; and

(*b*) to the legislature and government of each province in respect of all matters within the authority of the legislature of each province.

Exception

(2) Notwithstanding subsection (1), section 15 shall not have effect until three years after this section comes into force.

Exception where express declaration

**33.** (1) Parliament or the legislature of a province may expressly declare in an Act of Parliament or of the legislature, as the case may be, that the Act or a provision thereof shall operate notwithstanding a provision included in section 2 or sections 7 to 15 of this Charter.

Operation of exception

(2) An Act or a provision of an Act in respect of which a declaration made under this section is in effect shall have such operation as it would have but for the provision of this Charter referred to in the declaration.

Five year limitation

(3) A declaration made under subsection (1) shall cease to have effect five years after it comes into force or on such earlier date as may be specified in the declaration.

Re-enactment

(4) Parliament or a legislature of a province may re-enact a declaration made under subsection (1).

Five year limitation

(5) Subsection (3) applies in respect of a re-enactment made under subsection (4).

## Citation

Citation

**34.** This Part may be cited as the *Canadian Charter of Rights and Freedoms*.

## PART II

# RIGHTS OF THE ABORIGINAL PEOPLES OF CANADA

Recognition of existing aboriginal and treaty rights

**35.** (1) The existing aboriginal and treaty rights of the aboriginal peoples of Canada are hereby recognized and affirmed.

Definition of "aboriginal peoples of Canada"

(2) In this Act, "aboriginal peoples of Canada" includes the Indian, Inuit and Métis peoples of Canada.

## PART III

# EQUALIZATION AND REGIONAL DISPARITIES

Commitment to promote equal opportunities

**36.** (1) Without altering the legislative authority of Parliament or of the provincial legislatures, or the rights of any of them with respect to the exercise of their legislative authority, Parliament and the legislatures, together with the government of Canada and the provincial governments, are committed to

(a) promoting equal opportunities for the well-being of Canadians;

(b) furthering economic development to reduce disparity in opportunities; and

(c) providing essential public services of reasonable quality to all Canadians.

Commitment respecting public services

(2) Parliament and the government of Canada are committed to the principle of making equalization payments to ensure that provincial governments have sufficient revenues to provide reasonably comparable levels of public services at reasonably comparable levels of taxation.

## PART IV

# CONSTITUTIONAL CONFERENCE

Constitutional
conference

**37.** (1) A constitutional conference composed of the Prime Minister of Canada and the first ministers of the provinces shall be convened by the Prime Minister of Canada within one year after this Part comes into force.

Participation of
aboriginal
peoples

(2) The conference convened under subsection (1) shall have included in its agenda an item respecting constitutional matters that directly affect the aboriginal peoples of Canada, including the identification and definition of the rights of those peoples to be included in the Constitution of Canada, and the Prime Minister of Canada shall invite representatives of those peoples to participate in the discussions on that item.

Participation of
territories

(3) The Prime Minister of Canada shall invite elected representatives of the governments of the Yukon Territory and the Northwest Territories to participate in the discussions on any item on the agenda of the conference convened under subsection (1) that, in the opinion of the Prime Minister, directly affects the Yukon Territory and the Northwest Territories.

## PART V

# PROCEDURE FOR AMENDING CONSTITUTION OF CANADA

General
procedure for
amending
Constitution
of Canada

**38.** (1) An amendment to the Constitution of Canada may be made by proclamation issued by the Governor General under the Great Seal of Canada where so authorized by

(*a*) resolutions of the Senate and House of Commons; and

(*b*) resolutions of the legislative assemblies of at least two-thirds of the provinces that have, in the aggregate, according to the then latest general census, at least fifty per cent of the population of all the provinces.

Majority of members

(2) An amendment made under subsection (1) that derogates from the legislative powers, the proprietary rights or any other rights or privileges of the legislature or government of a province shall require a resolution supported by a majority of the members of each of the Senate, the House of Commons and the legislative assemblies required under subsection (1).

Expression of dissent

(3) An amendment referred to in subsection (2) shall not have effect in a province the legislative assembly of which has expressed its dissent thereto by resolution supported by a majority of its members prior to the issue of the proclamation to which the amendment relates unless that legislative assembly, subsequently, by resolution supported by a majority of its members, revokes its dissent and authorizes the amendment.

Revocation of dissent

(4) A resolution of dissent made for the purposes of subsection (3) may be revoked at any time before or after the issue of the proclamation to which it relates.

Restriction on proclamation

**39.** (1) A proclamation shall not be issued under subsection 38(1) before the expiration of one year from the adoption of the resolution initiating the amendment procedure thereunder, unless the legislative assembly of each province has previously adopted a resolution of assent or dissent.

Idem

(2) A proclamation shall not be issued under subsection 38(1) after the expiration of three years from the adoption of the resolution initiating the amendment procedure thereunder.

Compensation

**40.** Where an amendment is made under subsection 38(1) that transfers provincial legislative powers relating to education or other cultural matters from provincial legislatures to Parliament, Canada shall provide reasonable compensation to any province to which the amendment does not apply.

**41.** An amendment to the Constitution of Canada in relation to the following matters may be made by proclamation issued by the Governor General under the Great Seal of Canada only where authorized by resolutions of the Senate and House of Commons and of the legislative assembly of each province:

(*a*) the office of the Queen, the Governor General and the Lieutenant Governor of a province;

(*b*) the right of a province to a number of members in the House of Commons not less than the number of Senators by which the province is entitled to be represented at the time this Part comes into force;

(*c*) subject to section 43, the use of the English or the French language;

(*d*) the composition of the Supreme Court of Canada; and

(*e*) an amendment to this Part.

**42.** (1) An amendment to the Constitution of Canada in relation to the following matters may be made only in accordance with subsection 38(1):

(*a*) the principle of proportionate representation of the provinces in the House of Commons prescribed by the Constitution of Canada;

(*b*) the powers of the Senate and the method of selecting Senators;

(*c*) the number of members by which a province is entitled to be represented in the Senate and the residence qualifications of Senators;

(*d*) subject to paragraph 41(*d*), the Supreme Court of Canada;

(*e*) the extension of existing provinces into the territories; and

(*f*) notwithstanding any other law or practice, the establishment of new provinces.

(2) Subsections 38(2) to (4) do not apply in respect of amendments in relation to matters referred to in subsection (1).

Amendment of
provisions
relating to some
but not all
provinces
**43.** An amendment to the Constitution of Canada in relation to any provision that applies to one or more, but not all, provinces, including

(*a*) any alteration to boundaries between provinces, and

(b) any amendment to any provision that relates to the use of the English or the French language within a province,

may be made by proclamation issued by the Governor General under the Great Seal of Canada only where so authorized by resolutions of the Senate and House of Commons and of the legislative assembly of each province to which the amendment applies.

**Amendments by Parliament**

**44.** Subject to sections 41 and 42, Parliament may exclusively make laws amending the Constitution of Canada in relation to the executive government of Canada or the Senate and House of Commons.

**Amendments by provincial legislatures**

**45.** Subject to section 41, the legislature of each province may exclusively make laws amending the constitution of the province.

**Initiation of amendment procedures**

**46.** (1) The procedures for amendment under sections 38, 41, 42 and 43 may be initiated either by the Senate or the House of Commons or by the legislative assembly of a province.

**Revocation of authorization**

(2) A resolution of assent made for the purposes of this Part may be revoked at any time before the issue of a proclamation authorized by it.

**Amendments without Senate resolution**

**47.** (1) An amendment to the Constitution of Canada made by proclamation under section 38, 41, 42 or 43 may be made without a resolution of the Senate authorizing the issue of the proclamation if, within one hundred and eighty days after the adoption by the House of Commons of a resolution authorizing its issue, the Senate has not adopted such a resolution and if, at any time after the expiration of that period, the House of Commons again adopts the resolution.

**Computation of period**

(2) Any period when Parliament is prorogued or dissolved shall not be counted in computing the one hundred and eighty day period referred to in subsection (1).

**Advice to issue proclamation**

**48.** The Queen's Privy Council for Canada shall advise the Governor General to issue a proclamation under

this Part forthwith on the adoption of the resolutions
required for an amendment made by proclamation
under this Part.

Constitutional
conference

**49.** A constitutional conference composed of the Prime
Minister of Canada and the first ministers of the
provinces shall be convened by the Prime Minister of
Canada within fifteen years after this Part comes into
force to review the provisions of this Part.

## PART VI

## AMENDMENT TO THE CONSTITUTION ACT, 1867

Amendment to
Constitution
Act, 1867

**50.** The *Constitution Act, 1867* (formerly named the
*British North America Act, 1867*) is amended by
adding thereto, immediately after section 92 thereof,
the following heading and section:

### "Non-Renewable Natural Resources, Forestry Resources and Electrical Energy

Laws respecting
non-renewable
natural
resources,
forestry
resources and
electrical
energy

**92A.** (1) In each province, the legislature may
exclusively make laws in relation to
    (*a*) exploration for non-renewable natural
resources in the province;
    (*b*) development, conservation and management of
non-renewable natural resources and forestry
resources in the province, including laws in
relation to the rate of primary production therefrom; and
    (*c*) development, conservation and management of
sites and facilities in the province for the generation and production of electrical energy.

**Export from provinces of resources**

(2) In each province, the legislature may make laws in relation to the export from the province to another part of Canada of the primary production from non-renewable natural resources and forestry resources in the province and the production from facilities in the province for the generation of electrical energy, but such laws may not authorize or provide for discrimination in prices or in supplies exported to another part of Canada.

**Authority of Parliament**

(3) Nothing in subsection (2) derogates from the authority of Parliament to enact laws in relation to the matters referred to in that subsection and, where such a law of Parliament and a law of a province conflict, the law of Parliament prevails to the extent of the conflict.

**Taxation of resources**

(4) In each province, the legislature may make laws in relation to the raising of money by any mode or system of taxation in respect of
    (a) non-renewable natural resources and forestry resources in the province and the primary production therefrom, and
    (b) sites and facilities in the province for the generation of electrical energy and the production therefrom,
whether or not such production is exported in whole or in part from the province, but such laws may not authorize or provide for taxation that differentiates between production exported to another part of Canada and production not exported from the province.

**"Primary production"**

(5) The expression "primary production" has the meaning assigned by the Sixth Schedule.

**Existing powers or rights**

(6) Nothing in subsections (1) to (5) derogates from any powers or rights that a legislature or government of a province had immediately before the coming into force of this section."

**Idem**

51. The said Act is further amended by adding thereto the following Schedule:

## "THE SIXTH SCHEDULE

*Primary Production from Non-Renewable Natural Resources and Forestry Resources*

**1.** For the purposes of section 92A of this Act,
(*a*) production from a non-renewable natural resource is primary production therefrom if
(i) it is in the form in which it exists upon its recovery or severance from its natural state, or
(ii) it is a product resulting from processing or refining the resource, and is not a manufactured product or a product resulting from refining crude oil, refining upgraded heavy crude oil, refining gases or liquids derived from coal or refining a synthetic equivalent of crude oil; and
(*b*) production from a forestry resource is primary production therefrom if it consists of sawlogs, poles, lumber, wood chips, sawdust or any other primary wood product, or wood pulp, and is not a product manufactured from wood."

---

## PART VII

# GENERAL

Primacy of Constitution of Canada

**52.** (1) The Constitution of Canada is the supreme law of Canada, and any law that is inconsistent with the provisions of the Constitution is, to the extent of the inconsistency, of no force or effect.

Constitution of Canada

(2) The Constitution of Canada includes
(*a*) the *Canada Act*, including this Act;
(*b*) the Acts and orders referred to in Schedule I; and
(*c*) any amendment to any Act or order referred to in paragraph (*a*) or (*b*).

Amendments to Constitution of Canada

(3) Amendments to the Constitution of Canada shall be made only in accordance with the authority contained in the Constitution of Canada.

**Repeals and new names**

**53.** (1) The enactments referred to in Column I of Schedule I are hereby repealed or amended to the extent indicated in Column II thereof and, unless repealed, shall continue as law in Canada under the names set out in Column III thereof.

**Consequential amendments**

(2) Every enactment, except the *Canada Act*, that refers to an enactment referred to in Schedule I by the name in Column I thereof is hereby amended by substituting for that name the corresponding name in Column III thereof, and any British North America Act not referred to in Schedule I may be cited as the *Constitution Act* followed by the year and number, if any, of its enactment.

**Repeal and consequential amendments**

**54.** Part IV is repealed on the day that is one year after this Part comes into force and this section may be repealed and this Act renumbered, consequential upon the repeal of Part IV and this section, by proclamation issued by the Governor General under the Great Seal of Canada.

**French version of Constitution of Canada**

**55.** A French version of the portions of the Constitution of Canada referred to in Schedule I shall be prepared by the Minister of Justice of Canada as expeditiously as possible and, when any portion thereof sufficient to warrant action being taken has been so prepared, it shall be put forward for enactment by proclamation issued by the Governor General under the Great Seal of Canada pursuant to the procedure then applicable to an amendment of the same provisions of the Constitution of Canada.

**English and French versions of certain constitutional texts**

**56.** Where any portion of the Constitution of Canada has been or is enacted in English and French or where a French version of any portion of the Constitution is enacted pursuant to section 55, the English and French versions of that portion of the Constitution are equally authoritative.

**English and French versions of this Act**

**57.** The English and French versions of this Act are equally authoritative.

**Commencement**

**58.** Subject to section 59, this Act shall come into force on a day to be fixed by proclamation issued by the

Queen or the Governor General under the Great Seal
of Canada.

Commence-
ment of
paragraph
23(1)(a) in
respect of
Quebec

**59.** (1) Paragraph 23(1)(*a*) shall come into force in
respect of Quebec on a day to be fixed by proclamation
issued by the Queen or the Governor General under
the Great Seal of Canada.

Authorization
of Quebec

(2) A proclamation under subsection (1) shall be
issued only where authorized by the legislative
assembly or government of Quebec.

Repeal of this
section

(3) This section may be repealed on the day paragraph
23(1)(*a*) comes into force in respect of Quebec and this
Act amended and renumbered, consequential upon the
repeal of this section, by proclamation issued by the
Queen or the Governor General under the Great Seal
of Canada.

Short title and
citations

**60.** This Act may be cited as the *Constitution Act,
1981*, and the Constitution Acts 1867 to 1975 (No. 2)
and this Act may be cited together as the *Constitution
Acts, 1867 to 1981*.


[Author's note: Hereafter follows Schedule I,
which modernizes the constitution by updating
titles of earlier constitutional acts and by re-
pealing all or part of earlier enactments made
redundant by the new constitution.]

# Appendix 2
# Highlights of the Kirby Memorandum

[This document, dated August 30, 1980, was prepared by a group of government officials led by Michael Kirby and intended for "Ministers' Eyes Only." It was leaked by a federal official to the Quebec delegation just prior to the September 1980 First Ministers' Conference on the Constitution. It soon came into the hands of provincial delegations and the news media. In spite of the fact that their strategy was now known to the provinces, federal officials stuck closely to the options outlined in this document. It therefore offers valuable insight into the considerations behind the federal position, while providing a glimpse of the approach federal civil servants and politicians took to this issue.]*

## Introduction

This paper is intended to provide Ministers with a review and assessment of the summer's constitutional discussions, to propose positions and a strategy for the forthcoming First Ministers' Conference (FMC) on the Constitution, and to consider various courses of action for handling a constitutional resolution in Parliament this fall and other related matters.

---

*Square brackets indicate author's commentary.

For this purpose, the memorandum is divided into six main sections:

☐ An overview and general assessment of the mood of the constitutional talks at their conclusion,

☐ A status report of each of the twelve items on the constitutional agenda, including a proposed federal position at the FMC and a proposed strategy for the FMC,

☐ A review of the possible packages of constitutional reform which the government might place before Parliament this fall,

☐ An outline of strategic considerations in the post FMC period,

☐ A discussion of the continuing information program in support of constitutional renewal, and

☐ A concluding section.

[After a brief account of the mood surrounding constitutional matters in the summer of 1980, the Kirby memorandum reviewed the status of the twelve issues on the agenda: the federal stand on each, the provincial stand, and the proposed position to be taken by Ottawa at the First Ministers' Conference. This section concluded with a proposal for conference strategy. Selected portions follow.]

## Conclusions — Proposed First Ministers' Conference Strategy

The strategy which is proposed below is predicated on the assumption that the preferred outcome of the Conference is an agreement on the greatest possible number of issues. Such an agreement as far as the federal government is concerned must include as a minimum the elements of the People's Package. As far as the provinces are concerned, it is very clear that without agreement on issues of particular concern to them within the Package on Government Powers and Institutions, there will be no agreement on the People's Package alone. Therefore, any agreement can only be on a very large number of items.

While the federal government *must* maintain its position that elements in one package cannot be bargained against elements in the other, it must also understand in terms of its own strategy that the more it is possible to reach agreement in the area of Powers and Institutions, the easier it will be at the end of the day for the provinces to accept the People's Package.

There is a genuine fear amongst the provinces that the federal government is not interested in the Powers and Institutions Package. Much of the resistance to the People's Package has been to try to force the federal government to bargain within the Institutions and Powers Package.

The federal strategy from the beginning has been, and must continue to be, to demonstrate very clearly its interest in *both* packages and its intention to bargain *within* the Powers and Institutions Package. The federal government must make very clear that it understands that an agreement means that no one will be entirely happy on every item, but that everyone should be able to claim victory on something.

The strategy on the People's Package is really very simple. The federal positions on the issues within the package are clearly very popular with the Canadian public and should be presented on television in the most favourable light possible. The Premiers who are opposed should be put on the defensive very quickly and should be made to appear that they prefer to trust politicians rather than impartial and non-partisan courts in the protection of the basic rights of citizens in a democratic society. It is evident that the Canadian people prefer their rights protected by judges rather than by politicians. As far as patriation is concerned, the issue can very easily be developed to make those provinces who oppose it look as though they believe that they are happy with Canada's problems being debated in the Parliament of another country.

In private, the provinces must be told that there is absolutely no question but that the federal government will proceed very quickly with *at least* all the elements of the People's Package and that it would therefore be to their advantage to bargain in good faith on the other issues so that they too will be relatively satisfied after the Conference. It should be made abundantly clear that on Powers and Institutions, the federal government expects *give* from the provinces as well as *take*.

The CCMC meetings have probably laid the groundwork for a deal on Powers and Institutions. The federal strategy was to take the initiative and to put the provinces on the defensive. Yet the federal government demonstrated at the required moment enough flexibility to allow the provinces to save some face. The same strategy must be followed at the FMC.

A deal must include something for everyone. And this is now distinctly possible because the federal government has been able to maintain the initiative and has used extremely effectively its principal weapon which is the economic union item....

[All emphases in original throughout]

[The third section of the Kirby memorandum set out four alternative packages of items from which Ottawa is to choose, assuming that the September 1980 conference produced no agreement. This discussion is followed by a section setting out strategy options for the period following the conference. Included as one option was the approach actually taken by the government: a parliamentary resolution tabled in the House and sent to a special committee. Here is the account of this option.]

## 2. Start the Debate September 29, sending the Resolution to Committee when the Budget is Presented on or Soon After October 15

This option pre-supposes one of two circumstances:

☐ that there is a decision on the merits of the case that there should be a Committee stage;

☐ that, by prolonged and determined obstruction, the House makes the proposed extended sittings impossible, and hence a committee is forced on the government.

It is proposed that if there is reference to Committee there would be identical references in the House and Senate to a Special Joint Committee of the Senate and the House. It is to be expected that the House would not welcome (but would accept) a Joint Committee. It would probably please the Senate.

Whether or not there is reference to Committee, there should be no mention of such a reference in the Resolution when it is tabled. The debate should open on the assumption that there is only one objective, to bring the matter to a vote. From a tactical point of view, reference to Committee would best be made in response to Opposition demands.

*Advantages*

☐ If the Resolution is tabled September 29, the "dead time" between October 15 and January 15 would be avoided because the Committee would be sitting during this period.

☐ A highly contentious measure may be best contained in a Committee where it is more readily managed by the House Leader and his officers, and where easier and more effective relations can be maintained with the Press Gallery, since relatively few reporters will follow the proceedings.

☐ Interested individuals and groups can participate directly in constitutional renewal.

*Disadvantages*

☐ The reference debate (in the House at least) might be prolonged and difficult. Assuming a very hostile climate the Opposition would filibuster, knowing the budget will have to be introduced around October 15, and force the government to accept wide terms of reference, to permit the Committee to travel to all major centres in Canada, to hear all comers, and to set no time limitation. The situation would be eased if, as might be expected, the Opposition claim in the debate that the Resolution is extremely complex. The Committee route could then be put to the Opposition as a suitable means of dealing with a complex issue. It would still be likely that the Opposition would insist on an all-embracing reference, provision for travel, etc.

A committee, however set up, might come to see itself as a committee of inquiry, or a Royal Commission, labour for many months and produce a voluminous report that could be very difficult to cope with. Certainly some elements in the public would push the Committee in this direction.

In Committee the government's position is likely to suffer. Attackers would be louder and more numerous than defenders. Careful choice of government members would be essential, and careful orchestration of hearings would be needed to ensure effective presentation of the government's position.

[The Kirby memorandum showed that the government was well aware of the problems of proceeding unilaterally without the consent of the provinces. This document anticipated what proved to be the decision of the Supreme Court on the matter: that the federal government's uilateral action violated Canadian constitutional convention.]

## 4. POSSIBLE LEGAL CHALLENGES TO A UNILATERAL IMPLEMENTATION PROCESS

### 1. The Legal Position

As soon as the contents of a unilateral patriation package become known, upon introduction in Parliament, it can be assumed that opposition both inside and outside Parliament will focus more on the validity of the procedure than on the contents of the package and most likely will demand that a reference be taken to the Supreme Court before the resolution proceeds further in Parliament. It will be necessary to have a position on this matter at that time.

As to the question of validity, it is the view of the Department of Justice that a law passed by the U.K. Parliament to patriate the Constitution, with an amendment formula and other changes, could not be successfully attacked in the courts. It seems abundantly clear that the legal power remains for the U.K. Parliament to enact such a law for Canada, and it also seems clear that they will do so whenever so requested by the Parliament and Government of Canada.

The more troublesome question is that of the requirements of the conventions (i.e., practices) of the Canadian Constitution with respect to constitutional amendment. While the British convention is that the U.K. Parliament will act when requested to do so by the Canadian Parliament, there is a potential problem with the Canadian convention concerning the role of the provinces prior to such a request being made. An argument is already being advanced by Ontario that patriation with an amendment formula would involve a change of a fundamental nature affecting the provinces and that on the basis of past practices there is now a clear convention in Canada that such action requires consultation with, and the consent of, all provinces. This is based on the premise that the "unilateral" adoption of an amending formula would affect existing rights of the provinces, at least their "right" of veto over amendments. (*Unilateral patriation combined only with an amending formula requiring unanimity would, on this basis, not be assailable.*)

Further, it is argued that this convention would be enforced as a rule of law by the courts.

The main lines of argument against this case are:

(1) there is no convention clearly applicable to patriation by itself, and the relevance of conventions to the rest of the package would very much depend on its contents (the strength of our argument here would therefore vary with the contents);

(2) even if the unanimity convention applies, it has proven to be impossible to follow and therefore is no longer relevant (demonstrable after 53 years of seeking an agreed amending formula) (this is a stronger argument);

(3) even if there is such a convention, it is a Canadian convention only and cannot affect action by the U.K. Parliament (also a stronger argument); and

(4) in any event, conventions are not legally enforceable by the courts and do not limit the legal powers of Parliament (this is a very strong argument that is supported by the overwhelming weight of authority).

It may therefore be fairly safely assumed that if the question somehow came before a Canadian court, it would uphold the legal validity of the U.K. legislation effecting patriation. The court might very well, however, make a pronouncement, not necessary for the decision, that the patriation process was in violation of established conventions and therefore in one sense was "unconstitutional" even though legally valid.

Obviously, the foregoing suggests that while unilateral action can legally be accomplished, it involves the risk of prolonged dispute through the courts and the possibility of adverse judicial comment that could undermine the political legitimacy, though not the legal validity, of the patriation package. *This points up the desirability of achieving agreement with the provinces on a patriation package.*

[The Kirby memorandum demonstrates that Ottawa was paying close attention to public opinion on constitutional matters and was anxious to ensure public support for its actions. This concern went far beyond reading opinion polls. As the next excerpt shows, Ottawa considered in detail alternative advertising and propaganda strategies to push public opinion in the direction it wanted. It weighed the choice of "hard sell" versus "soft sell" with no apparent concerns except for what would work and what criticism its activities might generate.]

## 5. STRATEGIC CONSIDERATIONS VIS-A-VIS THE PUBLIC

To secure a maximum of public understanding and support, action to be taken after the First Ministers' Conference should appear to be a natural consequence of what has happened at that conference, not an abrupt change of direction nor a new start.

This places an admittedly heavy burden on the Prime Minister. It suggests that, while he strives for agreement, he must also shape and lead the deliberations toward *action*.

In other words, the public should *expect* implementation at the end of the conference.

This underlines the importance of the Prime Minister's closing speech which, in addition to making clear the outcome of the negotiations, should pave the way for the implementation phase.

Should the Prime Minister give a press conference after the FMC, both in his statement and in his answers to questions he may wish to continue to point the way toward implementation, stressing the future rather than the past.

Consideration should also be given to a major address to the nation on television and radio. The historic consequence of constitutional renewal is justification enough. The timing of such an address could be crucial. A possible date would be just before the House meets to debate the Resolution. (i.e., Sunday, September 28).

# V. CONTINUING INFORMATION PROGRAM — CONSTITUTIONAL RENEWAL

The purpose of this section is to facilitate discussion on the alternatives for providing the public with additional information on the constitutional renewal process, following the First Ministers' Conference.

It should be noted at the outset that federal government advertising and information initiatives to date have aroused considerable public interest in the issues being discussed, and have created a demand for more specific information. Thus it is essential to continue the process of communication to maintain the momentum and the climate for acceptance of change.

This section is designed to help Ministers decide:

(a) whether they want to continue an advertising campaign after the FMC; and if they do

(b) whether it will be a "hard sell" campaign aimed at promoting federal government initiatives, or a continuation of that "soft sell" used during July and August;

(c) whether the continuing communication program will be limited to standard information and public relations techniques (i.e. no paid advertising).

*The fundamental question to be addressed concerns the legitimacy of spending taxpayers' dollars to promote what will be deemed by many to be a politically partisan position.* Ministers may want to note that selling federal constitutional proposals is quite different from the Quebec referendum campaign, when all federal parties basically supported the government's position and hence did not object strongly to federal advertising.

Moreover, Ministers should recognize the important distinction between the use of advertising as a negotiating tactic and its use as a tool to sell the government's programs or policies over the head of the Opposition. During the summer, government advertising played a significant tactical role in two ways. First, it helped to keep the issue of constitutional reform before the public at a time when there was no other means for doing so since Parliament was not sitting. Second, it helped to persuade the provinces that the federal government was not bluffing; that it really did intend to take action this fall — unilaterally if necessary; and that to achieve this goal it was prepared to treat this round of constitutional negotiations more like a street-fight than a diplomatic negotiation.

But once the government has decided what action it intends to take, and Parliament has been reconvened to debate that proposed action, the role of advertising changes. At that point, public funds are being used to sell the governing party's position, yet such funds are not made available to Opposition parties. Thus, *the Opposition has no effective way to respond*, in contrast to the provinces which can (and did during the summer) respond by running their own advertising programs. *Under these circumstances, Ministers need to decide if advertising is politically legitimate.*

Moreover, even if a decision is made to proceed with advertising, there are several advertising strategies which are possible.

Keeping in mind that the shape and extent of future communications initiatives will be determined by the outcome of the FMC and the general strategy adopted by Cabinet to advance constitutional renewal, three alternatives are outlined below, along with an analysis of the advantages and disadvantages of each.

(Please note that the three alternatives are not mutually exclusive. This document assumes that Alternative C, the standard information and public relations activities, such as public speeches, news conferences, news releases, and distribution of publications, will proceed regardless of what decisions are taken concerning advertising. Either of the first two alternatives will reinforce and complement these traditional information techniques).

## A. Advertising — Hard Sell

*Advantages*

(1) An aggressive advertising campaign, using all media, is the most effective way of communicating the government's point of view to the majority of Canadians.

(2) Advertising is the only reliable way of countering provincial advertising (i.e., the hard sell campaign already started by the Government of Quebec, the threat by some Western provinces to do the same) and of most effectively correcting provincial and media misrepresentations of the federal position.

(3) Feedback from advertising done to date indicates that Canadians have received and accepted a rather soft message; they want something more concrete, they want more information. Advertising is the most effective way to meet this demand.

*Disadvantages*

(1) An aggressive advertising campaign will inevitably cause the government to incur considerable political cost in terms of strident criticism from Opposition parties in Parliament, from provinces and from the media.

(2) There is the moral dilemma, as noted previously, about committing large sums of the taxpayers' dollars to a campaign that many will see as being politically partisan.

(3) While there has been no discernible public outcry to date over federal constitutional advertising, it is quite possible that unfavourable public opinion could be stirred up when Parliament resumes and the Opposition parties step up their criticism.

**B. Advertising — Soft Sell**

*Advantages*

(1) Continuation of a "gentle" campaign would

provide the Opposition parties and some of the provinces with fewer grounds for strong criticism and it would continue to maintain a level of broad public interest in constitutional renewal.

*Disadvantages*

(1) The federal government would not be aggressively promoting its own constitutional initiatives.

(2) The government could be accused of spending a lot of money on vague generalities.

## C. Traditional Information and PR Practice

This alternative would involve the Prime Minister, Ministers and MPs making public speeches, holding news conferences, issuing news releases, distribution of published material.

*Advantages*

(1) It would offer no grounds for harsh criticisms from the Opposition parties or the provinces.

(2) It would not represent a significant and highly visible investment of public funds.

*Disadvantages*

(1) This is the least effective way of promoting whatever initiatives the Cabinet decides to take, in terms of reaching the majority of Canadians.

(2) While offering free factual publications is an important element of any information program, it reaches at best only a fraction of the population.

Attached, as Annex 2, for the information of Ministers, are scripts for two television advertisements.

One is an example of the "soft sell" approach used in Phase I of the constitutional advertising campaign. The other, which is more aggressive, was prepared for Phase II.

[The conclusion of the Kirby memorandum reviewed Ottawa's situation immediately prior to the September 1980 First Ministers' Conference. It accurately forecast that the conference probably would not lead to agreement, and underlined its recommendation of unilateral action by Ottawa should that failure occur. It concluded with the oft-quoted qualification that the fight would be rough, and rounded out this long presentation of options and proposals with a tag from Machiavelli, whose students the authors of the paper no doubt considered themselves to be.]

## VI. CONCLUSION

The summer of CCMC negotiations has created circumstances in which there is now a possibility of reaching agreement on a package of constitutional amendments. This possibility has developed largely because of the three key elements of the federal negotiating strategy:

☐ the statements that the federal government was going to take action this fall and would do so unilaterally if necessary. While this was initially not believed by most of the provinces, events of the last week (Mr. Chrétien's two speeches, the leaked Pitfield memo, etc.) have finally convinced them that the federal government is deadly serious this time. This conviction will cause several provinces to come to the FMC wanting an agreement, but for political reasons, needing in that agreement at least one item which they regard as being of political significance in their own province;

☐ the distinction between the People's Package and the Package of Government Powers and Institutions and, most importantly, the refusal of federal negotiators to bargain elements in one package against elements in the other. This, combined with the Gallup poll showing the popularity of the People's Package, and the insistence by federal negotiators that unilateral action would be on the whole package has led to closer agreement on a Charter of Rights than there has been before. The task at the FMC will be to broaden agreement on the Charter, in particular to get it to include language rights and mobility rights;

☐ the direct linking of Powers over the Economy (a new Section 121) with the resources item and the federal position that there would be no agreement on resources without agreement on Section 121.

Within the confines of maintaining these three key strategic principles, the challenge of the FMC will be to try to move the provinces toward an agreement recognizing that:

a) agreement will necessarily mean a large package since the provinces will not accept the People's Package on its own, and the federal government will not be part of an agreement that does not include the People's Package; in the light of these facts, an agreement on a broader package is clearly preferable to unilateral action on a smaller package provided that the larger package includes the elements of the People's Package;

b) the federal government must be seen to be negotiating in good faith, and to be trying hard to reach a negotiated solution, so that unilateral action is publicly acceptable if it becomes necessary;

c) the offer of an extension of FMC and/or a second round of negotiations on a new list of agenda items, is a key element in (b) but it ought not be offered until the very end of the conference when its purpose is to show the public that the federal government is prepared to walk the extra kilometre. Offering the second round too early would remove the pressure to reach an agreement because at the present time a key element in the dynamics of the negotiations is the fear provinces have that they will be stuck with the status quo on the economic items since, if the federal government is forced to move unilaterally on the People's Package, it might refuse to discuss key provincial issues for years to come;

d) an agreement is likelier to be reached if each Premier can return home and be able to say that he won something in the negotiations, even if what he won was very modest, or at the very least to be able to justify why he did not get all he wanted (which probably explains why some of the provinces significantly moderated their positions in some of their key issues this week).

The probability of an agreement is not high. Unilateral action is therefore a distinct possibility. *In the event unilateral action becomes necessary, Ministers should understand that the fight in Parliament and the country will be very, very rough.* For as Machiavelli said: "It should be borne in mind that there is nothing more difficult to arrange, more doubtful of success, and more dangerous to carry through than initiating changes in a state's constitution."

# Notes on Sources

## Introduction

The Trudeau quotations are taken from a transcript of his press conference in Seoul, South Korea, September 29, 1981. Lévesque's musings over anglophone assimilation can be found in the appendix of P. Desbarats, *René: A Canadian in Search of a Country* (Toronto: McClelland and Stewart, 1976).

## Chapter 1

The Trudeau quote comes from a letter to Premier Blakeney, September 13, 1978, in *Proposals on the Constitution, 1971-1978* (Canadian Intergovernmental Conference Secretariat, 1978), p. 26.

## Chapter 2

Quotes from the Kirby memorandum are from "Report to Cabinet on Constitutional Discussions, Summer, 1980 and the Outlook for the First Ministers Conference and Beyond," August 30, 1980, pp. 32, 59, 33, 60. Quotations from the first ministers are drawn from transcripts of the proceedings of the First Ministers' Conference, September 1980 (Canadian Intergovernmental Conference Secretariat, September 1980).

## Chapter 3

Quotes from the Kirby memorandum are from "Report to Cabinet," pp. 39, 40, 46, 49-50, 51. The Trudeau quote is from the "Statement of the Prime Minister," Office of the Prime Minister, October 2, 1980, p. 2. The evidence of the debate over unilateral action and the quote thereon are from Paul Gérin-Lajoie, *Constitutional Amendment in Canada* (Toronto: University of Toronto Press, 1950), p. 254. Joe Clark's remarks are taken from the "Statement by Rt. Hon. Joe Clark on the Proposed Resolution Respecting the Constitution of Canada," P.C. News Release, October 2, 1980, pp. 1-2. Those by Premier Davis are from "News Release, Statement on the Constitution in the Legislature," October 6, 1980. The quotations from the Kershaw report are from Great Britain, House of Commons, First Report from the Foreign Affairs Committee, 1980-1981 Session, *British North America Acts: The Role of Parliament*, p. xii. Justice Minister Chrétien is cited from Canada, House of Commons, Debates, February 17, 1981, p. 7373.

## Chapter 4

All quotations in this chapter are taken directly from the factums of the respective attorneys general or the Sept. 28, 1981, judgement of the Supreme Court on the Reference regarding the Amendment of the Constitution of Canada.

## Chapter 5

Quotations from first ministers are taken either from transcripts of press conferences, from direct interviews, or as reported by the *Globe and Mail* on the dates indicated. Those taken at the conference are from the "Transcript of the Federal-Provincial Conference of First Ministers," November 2 and 5, 1981 (Canadian Intergovernmental Conference Secretariat). The post-conference rhetoric is as quoted in the *Globe and Mail*, November 16, 1981.

## Chapter 6

Much of the material on bilingualism and the fate of minorities is from Richard J. Joy, *Languages in Conflict* (Toronto: McClelland and Stewart, 1972), but especially from his *Canada's Official-Language Minorities* (Montreal: C.D. Howe Research Institute, 1978), an update of the earlier study. The quotation appears on p. 33 of the latter work.